D1444197

In the *Uncommon* high school group studies, Jim Burns pulls together the key ingredients for an effective series. He captures the combination of teen involvement and a solid biblical perspective with topics that are relevant and straightforward. This will be a valuable tool in the local church.

dennis "tiger" mcluen
Executive Director, Youth Leadership (www.youthleadership.com)

Young people need the information necessary to make wise decisions related to everyday problems. The *Uncommon* high school group studies will help many young people integrate their faith into everyday life, which, after all, is our goal as youth workers.

miles mcpherson
Senior Pastor, The Rock Church, San Diego, California

This is a resource that is user-friendly, learner-centered and intentionally biblical. I love having a resource like this that I can recommend to youth ministry volunteers and professionals.

duffy robbins
Professor of Youth Ministry, Eastern University, St. Davids, Pennsylvania

The *uncommon* high school group studies provide the motivation and information for leaders and the types of experience and content that will capture high school people. I recommend it highly.

denny rydberg
President, Young Life (www.younglife.org)

Jim Burns has done it again! This is a practical, timely and reality-based resource for equipping teens to live life in the fast-paced, pressure-packed adolescent world of today.

rich van pelt
President, Alongside Consulting, Denver, Colorado

Jim Burns has his finger on the pulse of youth today. He understands their mindsets and has prepared these studies in a way that will capture their attention and lead them to greater maturity in Christ.

rick warren
Senior Pastor, Saddleback Church, Lake Forest, California
Author of *The Purpose Driven Life*

jim burns

general editor

prayer &
the devotional
life

Published by Gospel Light
Ventura, California, U.S.A.
www.gospellight.com
Printed in the U.S.A.

Opening introductions for units written by Jim Burns. Opening devotions for sessions written by Mary Gross.

Originally published as *The Word on Prayer and the Devotional Life*
by Gospel Light in 1994.

Library of Congress Cataloging-in-Publication Data
Uncommon high school group study & leader's guide : prayer & the devotional life /
Jim Burns, general editor.
p. cm.
Rev. ed. of: The Word on prayer and the devotional life.
Includes bibliographical references and index.
ISBN 978-0-8307-5479-3 (trade paper : alk. paper)
1. Prayer—Christianity—Study and teaching. 2. Spiritual life—Christianity—
Study and teaching. 3. Church work with teenagers. I. Burns, Jim, 1953-
II. Word on prayer and the devotional life.
BV215.U53 2010
248.3'20835—dc22
2010008460

Rights for publishing this book outside the U.S.A. or in non-English languages are administered by Gospel Light Worldwide, an international not-for-profit ministry. For additional information, please visit www.glww.org, e-mail info@glww.org, or write to Gospel Light Worldwide, 1957 Eastman Avenue, Ventura, CA 93003, U.S.A.

To order copies of this book and other Gospel Light products in bulk quantities, please contact us at 1-800-446-7735.

dedication

To Mary Perdue—thank you for your
friendship and years of partnership in ministry.
You are truly a blessing!

contents

how to use the *uncommon* group bible studies

Each *Uncommon* group Bible study contains 12 sessions, which are divided into 3 stand-alone units of 4 sessions each. You may choose to teach all 12 sessions consecutively, to use just one unit, or to present individual sessions. You know your group, so do what works best for you and your students.

This is your leader's guidebook for teaching your group. Electronic files (in PDF format) of each session's student handouts are available for download at **www.gospellight.com/uncommon/prayer_and_the_devotional_life.zip**. The handouts include the "message," "dig," "apply," "reflect" and "meditation" sections of each study and have been formatted for easy printing. You may print as many copies as you need for your group.

Each session opens with a devotional meditation written for you, the youth leader. As hectic and trying as youth work is much of the time, it's important never to neglect your interior life. Use the devotions to refocus your heart and prepare yourself to share with kids the message that has already taken root in you. Each of the 12 sessions are divided into the following sections:

starter

Young people will stay in your youth group if they feel comfortable and make friends in the group. This section is designed for you and the students to get to know each other better.

message

The message section will introduce the Scripture reading for the session and get students thinking about how the passage applies to their lives.

dig

Many young people are biblically illiterate. In this section, students will dig into the Word of God and will begin to interact on a personal level with the concepts.

apply

Young people need the opportunity to think through the issues at hand. This section will get students talking about the passage of Scripture and interacting on important issues.

reflect

The conclusion to the study will allow students to reflect on some of the issues presented in the study on a more personal level.

meditation

A closing Scripture for the students to read and reflect on.

unit I
communicating with God

Before I started this curriculum project, I asked more than 150 of my youth ministry associates to rate their preferences for topics in the *Uncommon* group Bible studies. The number-one requested subject was prayer. It's interesting to me that a regular part of most every youth meeting and every worship service is prayer, but we rarely ever talk about it in our youth groups, Christian schools or even family devotions. Yet as missionary William Carey once wrote, "Prayer—secret, fervent, believing prayer—lies at the root of all personal godliness."

I am really glad you picked up this study, because on the following pages your students—and hopefully you—will be introduced to the depth and breadth of the role prayer plays in our spiritual lives. It's hard to just talk about prayer without praying. That's why I have included many opportunities for prayer and worship throughout the study. Experiential education tells us to not just talk about it . . . but also to *do it*.

When all is said and done, prayer is simply communication with God. And there isn't anything you can do that is more important than helping your students begin or continue the process of building a relationship of communication with the Creator, Savior and Sustainer of their lives.

I'm convinced that most young people (and adults as well) only pray the "God give me" prayer. Most people have the elements of prayer all messed up. We spend the vast majority of our time and energy asking for things and telling God what to do. But true prayer is much more than asking.

Praise frees our spirit to be in touch with our Creator. Thanksgiving gives us a proper attitude. Confession and forgiveness give us a right relationship with God, and asking our loving heavenly Father for His will and guidance reminds us of the depth of His love for us.

If your students aren't familiar with praise, thanksgiving, confession, asking and listening, then this is your opportunity to teach them these key biblical principles. You are placing some of the spiritual secrets of the master teacher, Jesus, at their feet.

Although prayer was the most-requested topic from youth workers, I doubt the students would have voted it number one. At camp, the class on prayer usually has a handful of faithful while the classes on sex, drugs and rock 'n' roll is standing-room only. That's okay. This study won't automatically change that trend. However, our job in this study is to get young people talking with God, to keep them talking to Him and have them enter into a deeper form of communication than ever before.

Don't get discouraged if some of your students aren't ready for a deeper communication with God. You are still placing before them spiritual truths that "will not return void" (see Isaiah

55:11). Let me leave you with this great thought from Richard Foster:

> Healthy prayer necessitates frequent experiences of the common, earthy, run-of-the-mill variety. Like walks, and talks, and good wholesome laughter. Like work in the yard, and chitchat with the neighbors, and washing windows. Like loving our spouse, and playing with our kids, and working with our colleagues. To be spiritually fit to scale the Himalayas of the spirit, we need regular exercise in the hills and valleys of ordinary life.[1]

Note

1. Richard J. Foster, *Prayer: Finding the Heart's True Home* (San Francisco, CA: Harper Collins, 1992), p. XII.

what is prayer?

Devote yourselves to prayer, being watchful and thankful.
COLOSSIANS 4:2

The word "prayer" may bring reactions from the young people you teach that range from "I can't do it!" to "I never think about it." They may find it hard to believe that anyone *really* has a prayer life or relationship with God that goes beyond what they see in the outward action of church events.

Where could young people get such a notion? Could it be from the (gulp!) adults around them? They see us interact with each other and with them. But how do most young people *know* if an adult ever interacts with God? Sure, pastors and Sunday School teachers talk about God. Prayers are said at the beginning and end of every church activity. But all too often, prayer and intimacy with God are either dealt with in abstract terms or not at all.

Prayer is the power—the life-changing element—that creates passionate drive and immense change in the lives of people who seek God. We do it in private, and we're reluctant to talk about it. Why is it so difficult to make our prayer lives public? Are we afraid that our students (or we) will get too fanatic? Or is it that when it comes to talking about our experiences, we really don't have that much to talk about?

That's where this lesson begins. When your intimacy with God becomes so exciting that your excitement spills over into the information this unit provides, your young people will begin to learn and experience, not just hear!

If you want to see the students you teach light up when they talk about real answers God has given them to their prayers . . . if you want to see them realize that they can go way beyond the "Now I lay me down to sleep" level of prayer that paralyzes much of Christendom . . . if there is even a spark of longing in your heart to see God make your own prayer life more powerful, more intimate, more life-changing . . . then you're on the right track! Give God all He wants of your prayer life.

Adults who eagerly evidence that they have been with God, and who comfortably talk about His powerful answers to prayer in their own lives, will take intimacy with God from the realm of the theoretical to the actual for young people. You can be the adult who proves to your students by your own life that intimacy with God is possible, real and life changing!

Prayer is friendship with God.
Friendship is not formal, but it is not formless:
it has its cultivation, its behavior, its obligations, even its disciplines;
and the casual mind kills it.
GEORGE ARTHUR BUTTRICK

what is prayer?

starter

WHAT'S BLOCKING YOUR PRAYER LIFE? Below is a list of potential prayer blockers. How often does each stand in the way of great communication with God?

	Often	Sometimes	Seldom
Lack of discipline	❏	❏	❏
Not making prayer a priority	❏	❏	❏
Falling asleep while praying	❏	❏	❏
Hectic schedule	❏	❏	❏
Don't feel God's presence	❏	❏	❏
Guilt	❏	❏	❏
Lack of faith God is listening	❏	❏	❏
Doubting His existence	❏	❏	❏
Selfishness	❏	❏	❏
Frustration in prayer	❏	❏	❏
Daydreaming	❏	❏	❏

What are the top three blockers in your life?

    1. _____

       _____

    2. _____

       _____

    3. _____

       _____

Keep track of this list—today's Bible study will help you face down your blockers during the next week.

message

Before we do anything, it's a good idea to know exactly what it is we want to do. (You wouldn't try cave diving without knowing what it is first, right?) So, what is prayer? Simple: *Prayer is communicating with God.* Here's the not-so-simple part: Just like communicating with other people, there are rules of the road that make communicating with God more effective. Learning these guidelines will help you open the line with Him and keep it open. Rich, deep and effective prayer contains five elements:

    1. Praise
    2. Thanksgiving
    3. Confession
    4. Asking
    5. Listening

1. These elements come straight from God's Word. Read each
    of the verses below. Which of the five elements of prayer
    do you find in the verse?

    If we confess our sins, he is faithful and just and will forgive us our
    sins and purify us from all unrighteousness (1 John 1:9).

    Element of prayer:

    _____

    _____

    _____

    Give thanks in all circumstances, for this is God's will for you in
    Christ Jesus (1 Thessalonians 5:18).

    Element of prayer:

    _____

    _____

    _____

    Ask and it will be given to you; seek and you will find; knock and
    the door will be opened to you (Matthew 7:7).

    Element of prayer:

    _____

    _____

    _____

    _____

I will praise you, O LORD, with all my heart; I will tell of all your wonders. I will be glad and rejoice in you; I will sing praise to your name, O Most High (Psalm 9:1-2).

Element of prayer:

_____

_____

_____

_____

Then a cloud appeared and enveloped them, and a voice came from the cloud: "This is my Son, whom I love. Listen to him!" (Mark 9:7).

Element of prayer:

_____

_____

_____

_____

2. For each of the five elements, (1) write a definition, (2) describe why it is important, and (3) write a short prayer that demonstrates that element.

Praise

Definition:

_____

_____

_____

Why it's important:

_____
_____
_____
_____

Prayer of praise:

_____
_____
_____
_____

Thanksgiving

Definition:

_____
_____
_____
_____

Why it's important:

_____
_____
_____
_____

Prayer of thanksgiving:

_____
_____
_____
_____

Confession

Definition:

_____

_____

_____

_____

Why it's important:

_____

_____

_____

_____

Prayer of confession:

_____

_____

_____

_____

Asking

Definition:

_____

_____

_____

_____

Why it's important:

_____

_____

_____

Prayer of asking:

_____

_____

_____

_____

Listening

Definition:

_____

_____

_____

_____

Why it's important:

_____

_____

_____

_____

Prayer of listening:

_____

_____

_____

_____

3. Are all five elements of prayer necessary for a well-rounded prayer life? Why or why not?

_____

_____

_____

_____

4. Which element(s) of prayer do you need to emphasize in your life right now? Why?

_____

_____

_____

_____

_____

_____

dig

One really good reason to incorporate all five elements of prayer into our daily conversations with God is the all-too-human tendency to treat Him like a vending machine: Put your prayer in the slot and out comes a prize! God wants us to ask for what we need . . . but what does that mean, exactly?

Regina Hammond, a 37-year-old flight attendant, won $100,000 in a Colorado lottery game, on top of $50,000 she won the previous year the same way. And she's not finished yet. Her goal is the $1 million grand prize.

Hammond believes that prayer has paved her way to riches. "I pray to God to help me and He answers," she says.[1]

1. Do you think Regina Hammond will win the million dollars? Why or why not?

_____

_____

_____

_____

2. How do you feel about Regina's claim that she is rich because of prayer?

   ....
   ....
   ....

3. If prayer works, why don't all lottery players pray and win?

   ....
   ....
   ....
   ....

4. Should people pray to get rich? To win sports events? To
   be successful? Explain.

   ....
   ....
   ....
   ....

5. Some people feel lotteries are sinful and should be illegal. If
   that's true, why would God answer Regina's prayers to win?

   ....
   ....
   ....
   ....

6. Would you pray to win a lottery? Why or why not?

   ....
   ....
   ....
   ....

7. Check the items that you would feel comfortable asking
    God for:

    ☐   An *A* on a test
    ☐   Lots of money
    ☐   Getting a job
    ☐   A better complexion
    ☐   Winning a game
    ☐   New clothes
    ☐   Not to get caught drinking
    ☐   Getting a date
    ☐   Losing or gaining weight

8. Why is it okay to pray for the items you checked, as op-
    posed to the other things? What's the difference?

    ....

    ....

    ....

    ....

apply

Prayer gives us the opportunity to share our lives with God, just
like talking with friends and family allows us to share our lives
with them. When we are in communication with God, we begin
to see Him at work in our lives, shaping us into the people He
wants us to be. The flipside is that failing to communicate with
God often shuts the door to His work in our lives.

Even with loads of knowledge about the subject of prayer, the
truth of the matter is that the only way to improve communica-

tion with God is *to pray*. But praying can be intimidating until you've had some practice.

1. Name three ways that prayer can bring you closer to God.

    1. _____
    2. _____
    3. _____

2. How is prayer different from a face-to-face conversation?

    _____

    _____

    _____

    _____

3. Do you think the five elements of prayer can help you communicate with God more like you communicate in a face-to-face conversation? Why or why not?

    _____

    _____

    _____

    _____

4. How can prayer be a dialogue with God rather than just a monologue?

    _____

    _____

    _____

5. Do you hear from God in prayer? If so, how does He speak
    to you? If not, how can you can listen for His voice?

    _____

    _____

    _____

    _____

    _____

reflect

1. Read each of the following situations, and then consider
    ways the person can overcome his or her prayer blocker.

    Situation 1: Jayden wants to spend more time in prayer, but
    he doesn't know how to fit one more thing in his crazy
    schedule. Between early-morning band rehearsal, after-
    school tennis practice and homework, the only time he can
    think to pray is just before he goes to bed. The problem: He
    keeps nodding off mid-prayer. What can Jayden do?

    _____

    _____

    _____

    _____

    Situation 2: Marcie and Dana decide that a great way to
    pray regularly is to pray together, so they make an appoint-
    ment to video chat every morning for prayer. More often
    than not, however, Marcie and Dana find themselves chat-

ting with each other more than with God. What are some ways they can stay focused on God instead of themselves?

_____

_____

_____

Situation 3: When Stu prays, he spends most of the time begging God's forgiveness for not praying enough. He feels bad about praying so rarely . . . and his guilt makes him want to pray even less! How can Stu get out of this vicious cycle and get on with praying?

_____

_____

_____

2. Remember your top three prayer blockers from this session's starter? Write them below.

   1. _____

   2. _____

   3. _____

3. Write your personal "situation" for each of your top three blockers (use the stories in question 1 as examples).

   Situation 1:

   _____

   _____

   _____

Situation 2:

_____
_____
_____
_____
_____

Situation 3:

_____
_____
_____
_____
_____

4. Now give yourself some good advice. As you did for other people's situations in question 1, figure out a way to overcome each of your blockers.

Situation 1:

_____
_____
_____
_____
_____

Situation 2:

_____
_____
_____
_____

Situation 3:

_____

_____

_____

_____

_____

Are you prepared to overcome your blockers and practice praying this week? To get started, find a partner or a small group and pray together. Don't forget to pray each of the five elements: (1) praise, (2) thanksgiving, (3) confession, (4) asking, and (5) listening.

meditation

In the morning, O Lord, you hear my voice;

in the morning I lay my requests before you

and wait in expectation.

PSALM 5:3

Note

1. Adapted from "Woman Says Prayer Helped Her Win Lottery," *Headline News Discussion Starters* (Loveland, CO: Group, 1990), pp. 30-31. Used by permission.

praise and thanksgiving

Enter his gates with thanksgiving and his courts with praise;
give thanks to him and praise his name.

PSALM 100:4

Among the elements of prayer, praise and thanksgiving sound extremely spiritual. And they are! But praise is also the place in our prayer lives where we grab hold of the *spiritual* and the *actual* at the same time and see them in a vivid way. When we praise God, we stop and look at what God has done. Here before us are actual, visible answers from God, whether things He has sent or situations He has changed—provided by thoroughly spiritual means! That gives us reason to remember that He is good, far better to us than we would ever be to ourselves.

When we stop to consider God's goodness and the astonishing answers He has made to our prayers, what effect does it have on us? We are humbled and grateful at the amazing grace He shows us every day. We know we don't deserve even a tiny portion of this love. This opens our hearts to thankfulness.

Paul tells us in 1 Thessalonians 5:18 that it is God's will for us to give thanks in all circumstances. *All* circumstances! Does this mean being thankful when we are pulled over by a patrolman rather than ranting to ourselves as we drive away with a ticket? That's hard to swallow.

But that's precisely it—because the thing that's most difficult to swallow is our pride. Pride is the root of all other sins, the spawning ground for every kind of rebellion that makes our lives miserable and our hearts resistant to the gentle moving of God's Spirit. And when we find ourselves in what we see as trouble, we have two choices: We can drop our pride and let go of our own way, or we can grab for control even more desperately.

When we give thanks to God in any situation, we acknowledge both to God and to ourselves just who we are—little people who need Him—and who He is—the only One who can help us. We are humbled and ready to hear what He has to say to us.

God wants us to notice what He is doing and praise Him for it, not because He needs our praise but because He knows that it takes us to new levels of awareness of *Him* even in the midst of our daily business. Whether you praise God in song, in words from your heart or simply in unspoken joy, you are *with* Him in those moments. And that is the essence of relationship with the One who loves you and desires to have you close to His heart!

*The prayer of thanksgiving should be quite specific. . . . If we are
"thankful for everything," we may end by being thankful for nothing.*
GEORGE ARTHUR BUTTRICK

praise and thanksgiving

starter

PRAISE AND THANKS. The words "praise" and "thanks" are sometimes used interchangeably, but when it comes to our prayer life, it's helpful to think about them as separate, yet related, concepts. We give God *praise* for who He is and *thanks* for what He does. Praise is the purest form of worship. When we have an attitude of praise, we free our spirits to experience God's presence and free ourselves to live for Him. We focus on Him instead of ourselves.

Brainstorm as many reasons as you possibly can to offer God your praise. What is it about Him—about His character, His being—that is worthy of praise?

_____

_____

_____

....
....
....
....
....
....

Now brainstorm as many reasons as you possibly can to thank God. What is He doing—in your life, in your family, in your church—that deserves your thanks?

....
....
....
....
....
....
....

message

Thanksgiving flows naturally from praise, because once we begin to recognize God's presence and goodness, we also begin to see His hand at work in our lives—blessing us, guiding us and caring for us. As we practice thanking God for all He is doing, we become humble and full of joy.

Psalm 150 is a great hymn of praise and thanksgiving to God. Read each of the verses from this psalm given below, and then answer the questions that follow.

Praise the LORD. Praise God in his sanctuary; praise him in his mighty heavens (v. 1).

1. Where do we praise God?

   _____

   _____

   _____

2. Does our church find times every week to praise Him? How? Where? When?

   _____

   _____

   _____

   _____

Praise him for his acts of power; praise him for his surpassing greatness (v. 2).

3. What are "acts of power"?

   _____

   _____

   _____

   _____

4. If God already knows how great He is, why do we need to tell Him?

   _____

   _____

   _____

   _____

Praise him with the sounding of the trumpet, praise him with the harp and lyre, praise him with tambourine and dancing, praise him with the strings and flute, praise him with the clash of cymbals, praise him with resounding cymbals (vv. 3-5).

5. When the psalm was written, these were the instruments people used to praise God. How do you think music helps us praise?

_____

_____

_____

_____

Let everything that has breath praise the LORD. *Praise the* LORD (v. 6).

6. Why should everything that breathes praise the Lord?

_____

_____

_____

_____

7. What are three ways you can praise the Lord daily?

1. _____

2. _____

3. _____

Psalm 34 is another great hymn of worship and praise. What's especially interesting about this psalm is the context in which it was written. The Bible records that this psalm was written by

David "when he pretended to be insane before Abimelech, who drove him away, and he left."

The story of this event is told in 1 Samuel 21. Saul, the king of Israel, was jealous of David and wanted to kill him. But Jonathan, Saul's son and David's best friend, warned him about the plot, and David was able to escape to Achish (also known as "Abimelech"; this was probably a royal title). Achish, as it turns out, was the king of the Philistines. If you remember the story of David and Goliath, you know that the Philistines and the Israelites didn't exactly get along, so, in effect, David was fleeing to one of Saul's enemies for safety.

However, the plan didn't work out as David expected. Some of the servants of the king recognized David and said, "Isn't this David, the king of the land?" (1 Samuel 21:10). When David heard this, he got a bit nervous that it would be Achish who would end his life. In a very real sense, he had jumped out of the frying pan and into the fire.

So, how did David get out of this mess? Well, he pretended he was crazy. He acted like a complete madman, making marks on the doors and letting the saliva drip down his beard. It was a convincing performance, because Achish said to his servants, "Look at the man! He is insane! Why bring him to me?" (v. 14). So he had David released. David immediately fled and went to hide out in a cave called Adullam. It was most likely there that he wrote the psalm of praise to God.

Keep this story in mind as you read this psalm, and then answer the questions that follow.

I will extol the LORD at all times; his praise will always be on my lips. My soul will boast in the LORD; let the afflicted hear and rejoice. Glorify the LORD with me; let us exalt his name together.

I sought the LORD, and he answered me; he delivered me from all my fears. Those who look to him are radiant; their faces are never covered with shame. This poor man called, and the LORD heard him; he saved him out of all his troubles. The angel of the LORD encamps around those who fear him, and he delivers them. Taste and see that the LORD is good; blessed is the man who takes refuge in him. Fear the LORD, you his saints, for those who fear him lack nothing. The lions may grow weak and hungry, but those who seek the LORD lack no good thing (Psalm 34:1-10).

8. Psalm 34:6 states, "This poor man called, and the LORD heard him." What does this tell you that David did when he was in this situation?

9. In what way did the Lord save him out of all his troubles?

10. According to this psalm, how often should we praise the Lord?

11. Summarize, in your own words, what Psalm 34:1-10 and
    Psalm 150 teach us about praising the Lord.

---

dig

Over and over again, the Scriptures tell us to be thankful people.
No one can read the Psalms and not notice the theme of thankfulness running through the pages of that great hymnal.

Think for a moment: Who are the happiest and most fulfilled
people you know? Most likely these people are thankful, grateful
people. Rather than constantly wishing for more things or different circumstances, they are delighted by the blessings that they
already have.

Christians have so much to be thankful for, yet we all struggle
at times with being ungrateful servants in our Father's house.
Thankfully (ha!), God's Word also has some wise guidance for us
about how to up our thankfulness quotient, even during trying
times. For starters, the Bible tells us that *thankfulness is a choice.* This
is made clear in the apostle Paul's instructions to the Thessalonian
believers when he tells them to "give thanks in all circumstances,
for this is God's will for you in Christ Jesus" (1 Thessalonians 5:18).

1. According to this verse, when should we give thanks?

---

2. Reread 1 Thessalonians 5:18 and notice what it does *not* say. It doesn't say, "Give thanks *for* all circumstances." How is giving thanks *in* all circumstances different than giving thanks *for* all circumstances?

3. What circumstances are you dealing with right now that make it difficult to be thankful? What is one thing for which you can be thankful in that situation?

4. The apostle James went a step further than Paul when he wrote, "Consider it pure joy, my brothers, whenever you face trials of many kinds, because you know that the testing of your faith develops perseverance" (James 1:2-3). How is your difficult situation helping you to develop perseverance?

5. Even when circumstances seem to be at their worst, there is always one very good reason for giving thanks: "But God demonstrates his own love for us in this: While we were still sinners, Christ died for us" (Romans 5:8). Does God's

love, demonstrated in Christ's sacrifice, inspire you to be
thankful? Why or why not?

_____

_____

_____

_____

6. How can focusing on God's love as you face tough times
   help you to practice thankfulness?

_____

_____

_____

_____

apply

It has been said that all the praise we offer this side of heaven is
"just practice." That may be true, but practice is the only way to
get really good at anything!

1. Reread Psalms 34 and 150. What are three "praise principles" you can draw from these verses? How can you apply
   these principles to your prayer life?

   Praise Principle 1:

_____

_____

_____

_____

Praise Principle 2:

_____

_____

_____

_____

Praise Principle 3:

_____

_____

_____

_____

2. Praise is something we practice individually and together. What are some creative ways you can praise God with your church, youth group or small group?

_____

_____

_____

_____

3. When you praise, you turn your focus from yourself to God. Is this difficult for you? Why or why not?

_____

_____

_____

_____

4. How can practicing praise have a positive effect on other areas of your spiritual life (serving others, obeying God's commands, resisting temptation, and so forth)?

....

....

....

....

5. Pick three psalms of praise to read every day during the coming week.

   1. ....

   2. ....

   3. ....

reflect

It has been said that it's much easier to break a bad habit if you replace it with a good one. Are you ready to get in the habit of thankfulness?

1. Why do you think Christmas and Easter are special times of thanksgiving for Christians?

....

....

....

2. Do you think it's easier to focus on the negative than on the positive? Why or why not?

....

....

....

3. Why do thankful people tend to be happier people?

    _____

    _____

    _____

    _____

4. List seven things God has done—one for each day of the
    coming week—that you are thankful for. Set aside some
    time each day to give thanks for that blessing.

    1. _____

    2. _____

    3. _____

    4. _____

    5. _____

    6. _____

    7. _____

5. Look up Psalm 100:4 and write it below. If you're up for
    the challenge, make it your memory verse for the week!

    _____

    _____

    _____

    _____

meditation

I will praise God's name in song and glorify
him with thanksgiving.
PSALM 69:30

confession

"Woman, where are they? Has no one condemned you?"
"No one, sir," she said.
"Then neither do I condemn you," Jesus declared.
"Go now and leave your life of sin."
JOHN 8:10-11

We've all heard it: "That makes me sick!" The exclamation is usually accompanied by a "yuck" expression on the face and a tightness in the stomach. What "turns your stomach"? A disturbing neighbor? A radical or a racist? A prostitute? A biker? A drug addict? If we haven't named your particular stomach-turner yet, keep thinking. What makes you say "Yuck!" inside?

The Pharisees brought a woman caught in adultery to Jesus, no doubt making "yuck faces." She really turned *their* stomachs! Jesus' response was intended to help them get over such sickness, using the principle expressed in James 5:16: "Confess your sins to each other and pray for each other so that you may be healed."

Squatting in the middle of a crowd full of tense self-righteousness, He began to write in the dust. Perhaps He wrote names of women with whom the accusers had committed adultery; perhaps He wrote a list of other commandments they had failed to obey. Whatever He wrote gave the woman's accusers a chance to either confess their own sin and identify with the adulteress as fellow sinners or to walk away silent. They chose the latter.

Meanwhile, the woman was the picture of confession, for the whole world seemed to know about her sin. Utterly humbled and defenseless, she lay at the feet of the Lord Jesus. And what did He say to her? "I don't condemn you; go your way and sin no more!"

What does it take for us to be truly healed from our pride and self-righteousness? How do we get over our "turned stomachs" to notice our own sin? Confession. We confess first to God and then to others, and the forgiveness we receive releases the healing James described. The alternative is to walk away silent, letting the sin we hold eat away until it leaves a hole in our spiritual armor where Satan will send his darts to deeply injure us.

So we confess to God and to each other. What good does such healing do? Why does God want healed people anyway? James goes on to tell us why: because the fervent prayer of a righteous person is powerful and effective (see James 5:16). God wants righteous (spiritually healthy) people who can prevail in prayer. The battle going on all around us needs warriors who can pray with power!

God does not ask us to confess our sins because He needs to know we have sinned, but because He knows that we need to know we have sinned.

DICK EASTMAN

confession

starter

TRUE CONFESSIONS: Some things are easier than others to confess. Start easy:

Something very few people know about me is

If I could go anywhere in the world, I would go to

If I could do or be anything, I would

....

....

....

If I could choose a gift, I would get

....

....

....

My most embarrassing moment was

....

....

....

message

The stuff that is usually hardest to confess is our sin. If we feel embarrassed to admit when we've made simple mistakes, it's not surprising that we feel guilty and ashamed to admit when we've sinned. Below is a story from Jesus' life told in John 8:1-11 that offers a surprising twist on who should be ashamed and who needn't be. As you read these verses, consider the following questions: (1) What did the woman in the story do? (2) How did Jesus respond to the Pharisees? (3) Why did Jesus offer her forgiveness?

But Jesus went to the Mount of Olives. At dawn he appeared again in the temple courts, where all the people gathered around him, and he sat down to teach them. The teachers of the law and the Pharisees brought in a woman caught in adultery. They made her stand before the group and said to Jesus, "Teacher, this woman was caught in the act of adultery. In the Law Moses commanded us to stone such women. Now what do you say?" They were using this question as a trap, in order to have a basis for accusing him.

But Jesus bent down and started to write on the ground with his finger. When they kept on questioning him, he straightened up and said to them, "If any one of you is without sin, let him be the first to throw a stone at her." Again he stooped down and wrote on the ground.

At this, those who heard began to go away one at a time, the older ones first, until only Jesus was left, with the woman still standing there. Jesus straightened up and asked her, "Woman, where are they? Has no one condemned you?"

"No one, sir," she said.

"Then neither do I condemn you," Jesus declared. "Go now and leave your life of sin."

1. Put yourself in the adulterous woman's place. How would it feel to have your sin exposed to a crowd?

   _____

   _____

   _____

2. Now imagine that you are one of the woman's accusers. Even though Jesus did not get specific or recommend that they be stoned to death, He "exposed" their sin, too. How do you think that felt?

   _____

   _____

   _____

3. When the woman's accusers "admitted" their sin, they walked away. The woman, on the other hand, stayed with Jesus—and He forgave her. What do you think might have happened if the accusers had stayed, too?

_____

_____

_____

4. What the woman did—commit adultery—was a terrible sin, possibly worse than the sins committed by her accusers. Yet Jesus forgave her. Why were her sins forgiven while the accusers' sins were not?

_____

_____

_____

5. Are you holding on to a sin, instead of confessing and receiving forgiveness, because you are afraid of exposure? What do you find reassuring about the woman's story?

_____

_____

_____

_____

6. It's easy to focus on how disgusting other people's sins are in comparison to our own. List three celebrities and their sins that have recently been exposed in the media.

Celebrity #1: _____

His/her sin: _____

_____

_____

Celebrity #2: _____

His/her sin: _____

_____

_____

Celebrity #3: _____

His/her sin: _____

_____

_____

7. When you talk with your friends about celebrities' sins (or about other friends' sins!), how are you like the adulterous woman's accusers?

_____

_____

_____

8. What is one thing you can do to remind yourself that "all have sinned and fall short of the glory of God" (Romans 3:23)? ("All" includes you!)

_____

_____

_____

_____

9. The word "confess" actually means *to agree.* Confessing
    your sins to God is agreeing with Him that you, like every-
    one else, fall short of perfection. Read these verses on con-
    fession and forgiveness and discuss what they mean with
    your group or with a friend.

    1 John 1:9:

    _____

    _____

    _____

    Psalm 86:5:

    _____

    _____

    _____

    Isaiah 1:18:

    _____

    _____

    _____

    Hebrews 10:17:

    _____

    _____

    _____

dig

God provided a way for the ancient Israelites to confess their sins
and receive forgiveness. Some of the Old Testament (especially
the book of Leviticus) contains instructions for these rituals,

which emphasized animal sacrifice. Although the slaughter of animals may be sickening to contemplate in our day, the message is still clear: *Sin leads to death.*

Because the Jewish people were intimately familiar with the idea that pardon from sin requires a sacrifice, Jesus' death on the cross was a powerful symbol of God's once-and-for-all gift of forgiveness. The author of the book of Hebrews explains it like this:

> *But when the Messiah arrived, high priest of the superior things of this new covenant, he . . . bypassed the sacrifices consisting of goat and calf blood, instead using his own blood as the price to set us free once and for all. If that animal blood and the other rituals of purification were effective in cleaning up certain matters of our religion and behavior, think how much more the blood of Christ cleans up our whole lives, inside and out. Through the Spirit, Christ offered himself as an unblemished sacrifice, freeing us from all those dead-end efforts to make ourselves respectable, so that we can live all out for God.*
>
> *Like a will that takes effect when someone dies, the new covenant was put into action at Jesus' death. His death marked the transition from the old plan to the new one, canceling the old obligations and accompanying sins, and summoning the heirs to receive the eternal inheritance that was promised them. He brought together God and his people in this new way.*
>
> *Even the first plan required a death to set it in motion. After Moses had read out all the terms of the plan of the law—God's "will"—he took the blood of sacrificed animals and, in a solemn ritual, sprinkled the document and the people who were its beneficiaries. And then he attested its validity with the words, "This is the blood of the covenant commanded by God." He did the same thing with the place of worship and its furniture. Moses said to the people,*

"This is the blood of the covenant God has established with you."
Practically everything in a will hinges on a death. That's why blood,
the evidence of death, is used so much in our tradition, especially re-
garding forgiveness of sins (Hebrews 9:11-22, THE MESSAGE).

1. Why is the blood of Christ different from the blood of sac-
    rificed animals?

    _____

    _____

    _____

2. Leviticus 17:11 states, "For the life of a creature is in the
    blood, and I have given it to you to make atonement for
    yourselves on the altar; it is the blood that makes atone-
    ment for one's life." According to this verse, why is blood
    important?

    _____

    _____

    _____

3. Hebrews 9:22 says, "That's why blood, the evidence of
    death, is used so much in our tradition, especially regard-
    ing forgiveness of sins." Summarize, in your own words,
    how blood and forgiveness of sins are related.

    _____

    _____

    _____

Bestselling Christian author Max Lucado tells an unforgettable story of a mother and her four-year-old daughter. Susanna (the mom) and her daughter, Gayaney, were trying on clothes at her sister-in-law's home when the worst earthquake in the history of Armenia hit. There were 55,000 victims in this one quake.

They were on the fifth floor of an apartment building; the next thing they knew they had tumbled into the basement. Susanna and Gayaney were still alive but they were totally stuck and could not get up. "Mommy, I need a drink. Please give me something," was the cry of little Gayaney. Susanna found a 24-ounce jar of blackberry jam that had fallen into the basement. She gave the entire jar to her daughter to eat. It was gone by the second day.

"Mommy, I'm so thirsty." Susanna didn't know what to do. Truthfully, there was nothing she could do to help her daughter. They were trapped for eight days. Susanna lost track of time. She was cold and numb, and she lost hope. Periodically Susanna would sleep but usually awakened from the whining and whimpering of her precious daughter. "Mommy, I'm thirsty. Please give me something to drink." She then remembered that it was possible to drink blood! So she cut her left index finger and gave it to her daughter to suck. The drops of blood were not enough. "Please, Mommy, some more. Cut another finger." Susanna had no idea how many times she cut herself but if she hadn't, Gayaney would have died. Susanna's blood was her daughter's only hope.[1]

Max Lucado writes about this episode this way:

Beneath the rubble of a fallen world, he pierced his hands. In the wreckage of a collapsed humanity, he ripped open his side. His children were trapped, so he gave his blood.

It was all he had. His friends were gone. His strength was waning. His possessions had been gambled away at his feet. Even his Father had turned his head. His blood was all he had. But his blood was all it took.

"If anyone is thirsty," Jesus once said, "Let him come to me and drink. . . ."

And the hand was pierced.

And the blood was poured.

And the children are saved.[2]

4. What is your response to this story?

_____

_____

_____

_____

5. What does Jesus' sacrifice mean to you?

_____

_____

_____

_____

apply

Saint Peter's Square, May 1981, was the scene of a terrible event that shocked the world: an assassination attempt on Pope John Paul II. But the scene was quite different nearly three years later when Pope John Paul sat in Rome's Rebibbia Prison holding the hand of his would-be assassin, Mehment Ali Agca. The Pope forgave the man for the attempt on his life. What a tremendous story of forgiveness and reconciliation! As the Pope whispered quietly in that cell, he preached a message loud and clear to the entire world.

1. How would you feel about a person who tried to kill you?

2. How do you think the assassin felt after the Pope's message of forgiveness?

3. Can you imagine forgiving such an enormous offence? Why or why not?

4. It is uncommon in our world to forgive and forget—most of us are fond of holding grudges. Do you think it is possible to truly release someone from their debt to you? Why or why not?

5. Jesus said, "For if you forgive men when they sin against you, your heavenly Father will also forgive you. But if you do not forgive men their sins, your Father will not forgive your sins" (Matthew 6:14-15). Why do you think our forgiveness from the heavenly Father is dependent on our forgiveness of others?

_____

_____

_____

_____

6. Is there someone who has sinned against you whom you have not yet forgiven? What is keeping you from extending forgiveness to that person?

_____

_____

_____

_____

reflect

God has made a way, because of His love for us, to forgive our sins. He is ready, willing and able to forgive us the moment we confess. But He does not want us to stop with private confession, "just between You and me." Keep the story of the woman caught in adultery in mind as you read James 5:16: "Therefore confess your sins to each other and pray for each other so that you may be healed. The prayer of a righteous man is powerful and effective."

1. According to this verse, to whom are we supposed to confess our sins? Why?

   ....

   ....

   ....

   ....

2. Why do you think healing comes when we confess our
   sins to each other?

   ....

   ....

   ....

   ....

3. Have you ever confessed your sin to another person? If so,
   what was that experience like? If not, what has kept you
   from doing so?

   ....

   ....

   ....

   ....

4. How do you think confessing your sins to another believer
   could help you resist temptation in the future?

   ....

   ....

   ....

5. Do you ever have a hard time forgiving yourself for your sins? Do you think forgiving yourself might be easier if you confessed to another person? Why or why not?

6. Take a few minutes right now to write a prayer of confession. When you are ready, share it with a trustworthy Christian friend or pastor. Let the healing begin!

meditation

For I will forgive their wickedness and will
remember their sins no more.

JEREMIAH 31:34

Notes

1. Max Lucado, *The Applause of Heaven* (Nashville, TN: Thomas Nelson, 1996), pp. 94-95.
2. Ibid., pp. 96,98.

session 4

asking and listening

*If you then, though you are evil, know how to give good gifts
to your children, how much more will your Father in heaven give the
Holy Spirit to those who ask him!*

LUKE 5:13

There are many people who think that asking God for things is the main purpose of prayer. However, as we've seen so far in this study, prayer is far more than getting together with God to tick off lists of our needs and desires. Asking is only part of the larger picture of intimate relationship with God. But it is a viable and vital part of our talking with and listening to our Father. Jesus made it clear to us that we should ask God for everything we need, from our simplest daily needs like food to the thousands of dollars needed to fund a missions project.

In studying men and women for whom prayer was an integral part of their lives, we find that they never hesitated to ask God for the smallest (and what we might consider the silliest) things. If a shilling was needed to make up a payment, they prayed. If a pen was lost, they asked God to help them find it. But isn't this far too trivial for God?

Again, it's a part of the growing fabric of prayer that covers our lives as we live in closer intimacy with Him. Just as we find that our hunger for God increases as we feed on His Word more, so also we find that as we talk with Him more, we want to talk more with Him! We begin to discover that in the context of that daily closeness, it's really okay to ask Him for the smallest help, to invite His direction in the smallest detail.

As Jesus said, if we know how to give good gifts to our own children, how much more loving, how much more desirous to help us, is our infinitely loving Father! He wants to hear from each of us. Our perfect Father waits for us to come and be held close while we whisper our needs into His ear, perfectly trusting in our hearts that He will take perfect care of us! He delights to have His children tell Him what they need, nestling in trust against Him and secure in the knowledge that He will do everything for us!

As we hear Him respond to our petitions again and again, our desire grows to listen more closely for His voice of assurance and guidance. Just as in any intimate relationship, two-way communication draws our hearts closer to the Father.

God needs, greatly needs, priests who can draw near to Him,
who live in His presence, and by their intercession draw down
the blessings of His grace on others.

ANDREW MURRAY

asking and listening

starter

ASK AWAY: Deep, committed prayer consists of praise, thanksgiving, confession, asking and listening. Asking is the kind of prayer most people are familiar with. Even those who don't have a relationship with God have, at one time or another, asked "the Big Guy in the Sky" to bless or help them! So, with all you have learned about prayer in mind, answer the following questions:

Prayer is: _____

_____

_____

The best place for me to pray is: _____

_____

_____

The worst place for me to pray is: _____

_____

_____

The hardest thing about prayer is: _____

_____

_____

The greatest thing about prayer is: _____

_____

_____

message

Although communication with God involves much more than asking for things, Jesus made it clear that appealing to the Father for what we need is not just okay . . . it's what God wants! Read the following parable that Jesus told in Luke 11:5-13. As you read, consider the following questions: (1) Why was the man inside the house resistant to granting his friend's request? (2) What ultimately persuaded him to do so? (3) What was Jesus telling us about prayer?

> *Then he said to them, "Suppose one of you has a friend, and he goes to him at midnight and says, 'Friend, lend me three loaves of bread, because a friend of mine on a journey has come to me, and I have nothing to set before him.'*
>
> *"Then the one inside answers, 'Don't bother me. The door is already locked, and my children are with me in bed. I can't get up and give you anything.' I tell you, though he will not get up and*

give him the bread because he is his friend, yet because of the man's boldness he will get up and give him as much as he needs.

"So I say to you: Ask and it will be given to you; seek and you will find; knock and the door will be opened to you. For everyone who asks receives; he who seeks finds; and to him who knocks, the door will be opened.

"Which of you fathers, if your son asks for a fish, will give him a snake instead? Or if he asks for an egg, will give him a scorpion? If you then, though you are evil, know how to give good gifts to your children, how much more will your Father in heaven give the Holy Spirit to those who ask him!"

1. What characteristics did the friend at the door display that caused the person inside to finally open the door?

2. What is the point of Jesus' story?

3. In your own words, what does Jesus invite us to do in Luke 11:9-10?

4. What do you think keeps most believers from asking, seeking and knocking more often?

....

....

....

....

5. Why do you think Jesus compared the gifts of a good earthly father with the response of our heavenly Father?

....

....

....

....

6. How do the following verses influence your attitude about prayer?

Matthew 21:22:

....

....

....

Hebrews 11:1:

....

....

....

1 John 5:14-15:

....

....

....

dig

With the verses above in mind, write a letter to God. This is a chance to ask Him to meet specific needs in your life, in your family, in your church and youth group, and in the world. Here are some needs you might want to include in your letter:

- For the needs of your community, school, workplace

- For the needs of your church

- For the needs of missions, especially to unreached people around the world

- For your president and government leadership

- For the personal purity and lifestyle of your church leaders (Don't forget to thank God for them.)

- For your family (specifically and by name)

- For your own life—spiritual, mental, physical and emotional

When you are finished, put the letter in an envelope addressed to yourself and give it to your youth leader. He or she will mail it to you in three months, so that you can take an inventory of answered requests.

apply

If we really believe that communication is a two-way street, we must give God an opportunity to speak to us . . . because He will if we give Him a chance! There are many ways God speaks to His followers, including Scripture, the challenge or encouragement of other believers, the "still, small voice" of our conscience, dreams and visions, and Christian books, videos and music. What all of these different methods of communication have in common is the Holy Spirit; it is God living inside us who enables us to hear Him speak.

Just before His crucifixion, Jesus made this promise to His followers:

> *I will talk to the Father, and he'll provide you another Friend so that you will always have someone with you. This Friend is the Spirit of Truth. The godless world can't take him in because it doesn't have eyes to see him, doesn't know what to look for. But you know him already because he has been staying with you, and will even be in you! . . . when the Friend comes, the Spirit of the Truth, he will take you by the hand and guide you into all the truth there is. He won't draw attention to himself, but will make sense out of what is about to happen and, indeed, out of all that I have done and said. He will honor me; he will take from me and deliver it to you* (John 14:16-17; 16:13-14, *THE MESSAGE*).

1. According to this passage, what does the Spirit of Truth do in and for us?

    ---

2. Do you sense the Holy Spirit living in you? Have you experienced Him guiding you toward the truth? If so, what was that like? If not, write a prayer asking Jesus to fill you

with His Spirit. You may also want to talk with your pastor or youth leader about the Holy Spirit.

_____

_____

_____

_____

_____

3. The Bible; the challenge or encouragement of other believers; Christian books, videos and music; the "still, small voice" of our conscience; and dreams and visions were already mentioned as ways God speaks to us. Have you heard His voice through any of these? Which ones? What other ways has He spoken to you?

_____

_____

_____

_____

_____

4. Sometimes we don't hear God's voice because our thoughts and emotions are making too much "noise." In what ways have your mind and heart been too busy or loud to listen for God's guidance?

_____

_____

_____

_____

_____

5. What are some ways that you can quiet your heart and
   mind to hear from God?

   _____

   _____

   _____

   _____

6. How might praise, thanksgiving and confession help you
   focus your "inner ears" on the Holy Spirit?

   _____

   _____

   _____

   _____

reflect

Are you ready to start putting into practice all you have learned
about communicating with God? Say yes! Why? Because without
communication, relationships fall apart. Think about it: If you
never talked with your best friend again, could you keep calling
him or her your "best friend" for very long?

1. If prayer is so important, why do you think Christians
   pray so little?

   _____

   _____

   _____

2. Many believers have found that a journal is helpful for deepening their prayer lives. They write their prayers down, in addition to saying them aloud or silently. Why do you think a journal could be helpful? Have you considered using a prayer journal? Why or why not?

3. Other believers have found their communication with God deepening when they pray traditional prayers from the Church's long history. The most common example is the Lord's Prayer, which Jesus Himself taught to His followers (see Matthew 6:9-13) and which is still prayed daily by many Christians today. Do you use prayers written by other Christians? Why or why not?

4. What tools from this or the previous sessions will you use in the coming week to get praying?

5. Write a short prayer asking the Holy Spirit to strengthen and challenge you to deeper communication with God.

 meditation

Pray in the Spirit on all occasions with all kinds
of prayers and requests.

EPHESIANS 6:18

unit II
praying like Jesus

We talk all the time in church circles about "becoming Christ-like." We ask, "What would Jesus do?" (or wear "WWJD" T-shirts, wristbands and other gear). We talk about "imitating Christ." These phrases are fine shorthand for a central concept of the Christian life—as long as youth leaders, parents and other adults work to make clear to teens what they mean.

We know these phrases aren't just meaningless code, but do the youth whom we are trying to grow in the faith know? I like this unit of study so much because it takes seriously the idea that Jesus is our ultimate model for spiritual disciplines, especially the discipline of prayer.

We read in the Gospels that Jesus was a pray-er of uncompromising regularity. Luke tells us that He "often withdrew to lonely places and prayed" (5:16). His habits impressed His disciples:

"One day Jesus was praying in a certain place. When he finished, one of his disciples said to him, 'Lord, teach us to pray, just as John taught his disciples'" (Luke 11:1). If they could help it, they didn't want to miss out on a close relationship like Jesus was cultivating with the Father!

Of course, we call the prayer He taught the disciples "the Lord's Prayer," and this unit helps you introduce Jesus' prayer model to your youth. You'll also guide them to explore "the prayer of relinquishment" (Jesus modeled surrender to the Father's will in the Garden of Gethsemane) and how to intercede for others (as Jesus did during His last hours with the disciples). You'll also wrestle with your teens' questions about God's answers to prayer—which can sometimes feel like no answer at all.

In a culture where teens are enticed and even manipulated to imitate celebrities, sports stars and "artists" who are hardly worth the attention, what a privilege to point young people to the Lord. As you encourage and inspire the teens in your group through your own focus on Jesus, be confident that you are helping them orient their lives toward the only One worthy of imitation!

the Lord's prayer

This, then, is how you should pray: "Our Father in heaven, hallowed be your name, your kingdom come, your will be done on earth as it is in heaven. Give us today our daily bread. Forgive us our debts, as we also have forgiven our debtors. And lead us not into temptation, but deliver us from the evil one."

MATTHEW 6:9-13

We've heard the homily for years: Prayer changes things. It seems like an innocent idea. There's probably no doubt in our minds that prayer does change things. But the question is, what "things" does prayer change? Is prayer a celestial slot machine, where if we can just get the right combination of words and earnestness, God will change His mind and grant us that new Mercedes?! Or instead, might prayer change things we didn't want changed?

Prayer is the communion, the passion that makes the most enormous changes known to heaven and earth. But those changes usually come in a different way than we might expect: The changes must come in *us* first! As we learn to pray the kind of prayer Jesus taught, we find that it's more than a pattern for expression; His prayer is a pattern for new attitudes, for reordering our priorities according to the rule of God's kingdom. When we tell God that we want His will to be done in our lives the way it is done in heaven, we are pledging a staggering amount of obedience. When we ask that we be forgiven in the way we have forgiven others, we must stop to peel back our layers of righteousness to check for unresolved situations and unforgiven people.

This is change, all right! And this kind of change could be dangerous indeed. For Jesus' kind of prayer requires us to let go of our way completely. It requires us to be open to God's Spirit, to letting Him change our minds, retake our will and refocus our thinking. It leads us to freely lay our dearest hopes and our best ideas on the altar of God's desire for us, willing to slay them if He asks it.

When we begin to pray with our hearts as well as our lips, "Your will be done on earth as it is in heaven" (Matthew 6:10), we will find that prayer changes things indeed—by changing us completely.

Every Christian ought to say to the Savior as humbly as [the disciples]:
"Lord, teach us to pray." Ah! if we were only convinced of our ignorance
and of our need of a Teacher like Jesus Christ.

JEAN-NICHOLAS GROU

the Lord's prayer

starter

PRAYER TO ME: What is prayer like for you? For each pair of words or phrases below, choose which one most accurately describes your experience of prayer. When you're done, pick one of the pairs and write about why you picked that option.

Prayer to me is more like _____ than _____.

a window	a closet
listening	talking
making a friend	seeing an old friend
hard work	time of rest
journey inward	journey outward
discipline	spontaneity

message

The most famous prayer in Scripture is what we often call the Lord's Prayer. Many Christian denominations repeat this prayer every week in their services, and some even encourage their congregants to say it daily. The beauty, intensity and significance of this prayer of Jesus is unequaled in Scripture. As you read this model for prayer that Jesus gave to His disciples in Matthew 6:9-13, consider the following questions: (1) How did Jesus address God the Father? (2) What are the main requests to God in this prayer? (3) What does this model tell us about the way we should pray?

> *Our Father in heaven,*
>> *hallowed be your name,*
>> *your kingdom come,*
>> *your will be done*
>> *on earth as it is in heaven.*
> *Give us today our daily bread.*
>> *Forgive us our debts,*
>> *as we also have forgiven our debtors.*
> *And lead us not into temptation,*
>> *but deliver us from the evil one*

1. What is significant about the way that Jesus addressed the Father?

_____

_____

_____

_____

2. What does it mean for God's will to be done on earth as in heaven?

3. How did Jesus demonstrate God's will being done on earth, in His life, ministry, death and resurrection?

4. What needs did Jesus ask the Father to meet in His prayer?

5. In your own words, write each line of the Lord's Prayer.

    Our Father in heaven:

Hallowed be your name:

Your kingdom come:

Your will be done:

On earth as it is in heaven:

Give us today our daily bread:

Forgive us our debts:

_____

_____

_____

_____

As we also have forgiven our debtors:

_____

_____

_____

And lead us not into temptation:

_____

_____

_____

_____

But deliver us from the evil one:

_____

_____

_____

_____

dig

Read the conversation below with a friend or group. When you're finished, answer a few questions about your response.

if God should speak

Student: "Our Father, which art in heaven . . ."

God: Yes?

Student: Don't interrupt me. I'm praying.

God: But you called Me.

Student: Called You? I didn't call You. I'm praying. "Our Father which art in heaven . . ."

God: There, you did it again.

Student: Did what?

God: Called Me. You said, "Our Father which art in heaven." Here I am. What's on your mind?

Student: But I didn't mean anything by it. I was, you know, just saying my prayers for the day. I always say the Lord's Prayer. It makes me feel good, kind of like getting a duty done.

God: All right. Go on!

Student: "Hallowed be Thy name . . ."

God: Hold it! What do you mean by that?

Student: By what?

God: By "Hallowed be Thy name"?

Student: It means . . . it means . . . good grief! I don't know what it means! How should I know? It's just part of the prayer. By the way, what does it mean?

God: "Hallowed" means honored, holy, wonderful.

Student: Hey, that makes sense. I never thought about what hallowed means before. "Thy kingdom come, Thy will be done, on earth as it is in heaven."

God: Do you really mean that?

Student: Sure, why not?

God: What are you doing about it?

Student: Doing? Nothing, I guess. I just think it would be kind of neat if You got control of everything down here like You have up there.

God: Have I got control of you?

Student: Well, I go to church.

God: That isn't what I asked. What about that habit of lying? And your temper? You've got a problem there, you know. Then there's the way you spend money . . . all on yourself. And what about the kind of books you read?

Student: Stop picking on me! I'm just as good as some of the rest of those people—those phonies—at church!

God: Excuse me! I thought you were praying for My will to be done. If that's to happen, it will have to start with the ones who are praying for it. Like you, for example.

Student: Oh, all right. I guess. I do have some problems, some hang-ups. Now that You mention it, I could probably name some others.

God: So could I.

Student: I haven't thought about it very much until now, but I really would like to cut out some of those things. I would like to, you know, be really free.

God: Good! Now we're getting somewhere. We'll work together, you and I. Some victories can truly be won; I'm proud of you!

Student: Look, Lord! I need to finish up here. This is taking a lot longer than it usually does. "Give us this day our daily bread."

God: You need to cut out some of that "bread." You're overweight as it is.

Student: Hey, wait a minute! What is this, Criticize Me Day? Here I was doing my religious duty, and all of a sudden You break in and remind me of all my problems and shortcomings.

God: Prayer is a dangerous thing. You could wind up changed, you know. That's what I'm trying to get across to you. You called me, and here I am. It's too late to stop now. Keep on praying. I'm interested in the next part of your prayer. . . . Well, go on!

Student: I'm afraid to.

God: Afraid? Afraid of what?

Student: I know what You'll say next.

God: Try Me and see.

Student: "Forgive us our trespasses, as we forgive those who trespass against us."

God: What about Joe?

Student: I knew it! See, I knew You would bring him up! Lord, Joe has told lies about me, and cheated me out of some money, and he is the biggest phony around. He never paid back that debt he owes me. I have sworn to get even with him and then never associate with him again!

God: But your prayer! What about your prayer?

Student: I didn't mean it.

God: Well, at least you're honest. But it's not much fun carrying that load of bitterness around inside you, is it?

Student: No, but I'll feel better as soon as I get even. Boy, have I got some plans for old Joe! He'll wish he never did me any harm.

God: You won't feel any better. You'll only feel worse. Revenge isn't sweet. Think of how unhappy you are already. But I can change all that.

Student: You can? How?

God: Forgive Joe. Then the hate and sin will be Joe's problem, not yours. You may lose the money, but you will have settled your heart.

Student: But, Lord, I can't forgive Joe.

God: Then how do you expect Me to forgive you?

Student: Oh, You're right! You always are! More than I want revenge on Joe, I want to be right with You. All right, I forgive him. Lord, You help him find the right road in life. He's bound to be awfully miserable, now that I think about it. Anybody who goes around doing some of the things he does to others has to be out of it. Someway, somehow, show him the right way. Maybe You can even help me to help him?

God: There now! Wonderful! How do you feel?

Student: Hmmm! Well, not bad. Not bad at all. In fact, I feel pretty great! You know, I don't think I'll go to bed uptight tonight for the first time since I can remember. Maybe I won't be so tired from now on because I'm not getting enough rest.

God: You're not through with your prayer. Go on!

Student: Oh, all right. "And lead us not into temptation, but deliver us from evil."

God: Good! Good! I'll do that. Just don't put yourself in a place where you can be tempted.

Student: What do You mean?

God: Change some of your friendships. Some of your so-called friends are beginning to get to you. Don't be fooled! They advertise that they're having fun, but for you it could be ruin. Either you are going to have to stop being with them, or start being a positive influence on their lives. Don't use Me as an escape hatch!

Student: I don't understand.

God: Sure you do. You've done it a lot of times. You get caught in a bad situation. You get into trouble by not listening to Me, and then once you do, you come running to Me saying, "Lord, help me out of this mess, and I promise I'll never do it again." You remember some of those bargains you've tried to make with Me, don't you?

Student: Yes, I do. And I'm ashamed, Lord. I really am.

God: Which bargain are you remembering?

Student: When the woman next door saw me coming out of that NC-17 movie with my friends. I'd told my mother we were going to the mall. I remember telling You, "Oh, God, don't let her tell my mother where I've been." I promised to be in church every Sunday.

God: She didn't tell your mother, but you didn't keep your promise, did you?

Student: I'm sorry, Lord, I really am. Up until now, I thought that if I just prayed the Lord's Prayer every day then I could do what I liked. I didn't expect anything like this to happen.

God: Go ahead and finish your prayer!

Student: "For Thine is the kingdom, and the power and the glory, forever. Amen."

God: Do you know what would bring Me glory? What would make Me really happy?

Student: No, but I'd like to know. I want to please You. I know what a difference it can make in my life. I can see what a mess I've made of my life, and I can see how great it would be to really be one of Your followers.

God: You just answered My question.

Student: I did?

God: Yes. The thing that would bring Me glory is to have people like you truly love Me. And I see that happening between us now. Now that these old sins are exposed and out of the way . . . well, there's no telling what we can do together.

Student: Lord, let's see what we can make of me and my life, okay?

God: Yes, let's see![2]

1. What would you do if God broke into your prayer like this?

2. What is one thing that would change if God's will was done in your life the way it is in heaven?

3. Are you extending forgiveness as God forgives you? Why or why not?

4. What is so hard about forgiving those who sin against you? What is easy about it?

5. Do you sometimes lead *yourself* into evil? How can you better listen to God's voice and avoid getting into those tempting situations?

6. How will you bring glory and honor to God in the coming week?

apply

1. Take the inventory below to discover in which areas your prayer life needs some strengthening. Circle the number you think best indicates where you are now with prayer.[3]

Adoration: "Our Father in heaven, hallowed be your name." I spend time praising God for who He is: the sovereign Lord and ruler of the universe who cares about me personally, as though I am the only person in the world.

1	2	3	4	5	6	7	8	9	10

I'm Weak Here   I'm Strong Here

Intercession: "Your kingdom come, your will be done on earth as it is in heaven." I spend time praying about the needs of the world. I try to look at the world the way God looks at it and pray about the things that are on His heart.

1	2	3	4	5	6	7	8	9	10

I'm Weak Here   I'm Strong Here

Asking: "Give us today our daily bread." When I ask for myself, I ask simply for the necessities of life—food, shelter and contentment—mindful that there are so many in the world without these.

1	2	3	4	5	6	7	8	9	10

I'm Weak Here   I'm Strong Here

Forgiveness: "Forgive us our debts, as we also have forgiven our debtors." In my prayer time, I consciously recall the relationships in my family and with my associates where I have been hurt or hurt others and ask for forgiveness.

1	2	3	4	5	6	7	8	9	10

I'm Weak Here   I'm Strong Here

Temptation: "And lead us not into temptation, but deliver us from the evil one." In my prayer time, I allow God to speak to me about the areas where I am struggling or treading on dangerous ground.

1	2	3	4	5	6	7	8	9	10

I'm Weak Here   I'm Strong Here

2. How can the Lord's Prayer become nothing more than an everyday ritual, rather than a meaningful conversation with the Father?

_____

_____

_____

_____

3. What are some ways to keep the Lord's Prayer fresh and significant in your spiritual life?

_____

_____

_____

_____

4. Why do you think our forgiveness from the Father is conditional on our forgiving other people?

_____

_____

_____

_____

reflect

1. What attitudes, requests and priorities do you find in the
    Lord's Prayer?

    Attitudes:

    _____

    _____

    _____

    _____

    Requests:

    _____

    _____

    _____

    _____

    Priorities:

    _____

    _____

    _____

    _____

2. How can you more closely align your attitudes, requests
    and priorities with Jesus' model?

    Attitudes:

    _____

    _____

    _____

Requests:

_____

_____

_____

_____

Priorities:

_____

_____

_____

3. How will you bring glory and honor to God during the
   coming week?

_____

_____

_____

_____

meditation

For if you forgive men when they sin against you,

your heavenly Father will also forgive you.

MATTHEW 6:14

Notes
1. Adapted from *The Serendipity Bible Study Book* (Grand Rapids, MI: Zondervan, 1986), p. 33.
   Used by permission.
2. Adapted from Walt Kukkonen, "If God Should Speak," *Ideas 23* (El Cajon, CA: Youth Special-
   ties, 1980), pp. 35-39. Used by permission.
3. Adapted from *The Serendipity Bible Study Book* (Grand Rapids, MI: Zondervan, 1986), p. 33.
   Used by permission.

the prayer of relinquishment

He went away a second time and prayed,
"My Father, if it is not possible for this cup to be taken away unless
I drink it, may your will be done."

MATTHEW 26:42

Negotiation is a way of life for most of us. We give a little. The other party gives a little. Everyone is satisfied. This is the way the world works. It is not, however, the way God works! God is not the Great Negotiator in the Sky. His love is unconditional. His holiness is complete and perfect. And His demands are absolute.

There was once a woman who tried desperately to negotiate with God. She was willing to give Him everything but 5 percent. "Just 5 percent!" became her mental battle cry. After all, she was teaching Sunday School, helping with the youth group, taking her turn at nursery duty, organizing fund-raisers . . . and the list went on and on. But God simply does not negotiate. He did not want her Christian activity, her busyness. He wanted *all of her.* Ninety-five percent was not enough. And trying to hold on to that 5 percent nearly destroyed her.

"Absolute surrender" is a term we don't hear very often anymore, simply because the world views negotiation as a great good—which it is, in its place. Its place, however, is not with God. Absolute surrender of every single thing we are—what we hope, dream or want—must be laid at His feet. This is not a one-shot deal, either. It has less to do with one trip to the altar than with saying every single day, "God, I am Yours. All I have, all I want to keep for myself, that little 5 percent, is Yours. I take my hands off completely. Do what pleases You!" This is what God asks. Because when you are completely surrendered, His Spirit can move in and make you able to grow fruit and flow with love as was never possible with that 95 percent loaded up with Christian busyness!

What keeps you from absolute surrender? Whatever it is, give it up. Until you have made that step, in all honesty and humility, you will not be able to teach it to your students. The struggle is worth it and the result is glorious!

The self of instinct has missed its way. It carries a load of sin,
of lust, of dishonesty, of falsehood, of physical heredity which from God's
viewpoint is enmity to him. [In the prayer of Gethsemane]
all this Christ resolutely flung aside.
TOYOHIKO KAGAWA

the prayer of relinquishment

starter

WHOSE PRIORITIES? If you had only a few days to live, what would you do with your time? Choose one or more of the following and tell why.

- ❏ Throw a party
- ❏ Watch television
- ❏ Spend time with my family or closest friends
- ❏ Travel to a place I have always wanted to go
- ❏ Do nothing different
- ❏ Work hard to meet a girlfriend or boyfriend
- ❏ Plan my funeral
- ❏ Pray like crazy
- ❏ Other: _____

Note: You can download this group study guide in 8¹/₂" x 11¹/₂" format at **www.gospellight.com/uncommon/prayer and the devotional life.zip**

Before you go on, spend a few minutes thinking about your priorities. How do you determine what is most important to you? How does God factor in to your decisions about what is most important in your life?

message

Phrases like "What would Jesus do?" and "Be like Christ" are thrown around a lot in Christian circles—so often that we sometimes forget to be surprised by them. But if you think about it, the fact that followers of Jesus are called to become more and more like Him as they mature is totally shocking.

The apostle Paul wrote, "You were taught, with regard to your former way of life, to put off your old self, which is being corrupted by its deceitful desires; to be made new in the attitude of your minds; and to put on the new self, created to be like God in true righteousness and holiness" (Ephesians 4:22-24). As God's Spirit works in us, we become less like our sinful selves and more like Him. Take a moment to be amazed. (If you're not even a little bit shocked, you might want to check your pulse!)

If we are created to grow into Christ's righteousness and holiness, it's a good idea to study His example. We can find one such example in Matthew 26:36-46. As you read this passage, keep the following questions in mind: (1) How did Jesus interact with people? (2) How did He interact with God? (3) Why was prayer so important to Him?

Then Jesus went with his disciples to a place called Gethsemane, and he said to them, "Sit here while I go over there and pray." He took Peter and the two sons of Zebedee along with him, and he began to be sorrowful and troubled. Then he said to them, "My soul is overwhelmed with sorrow to the point of death. Stay here and keep watch with me."

Going a little farther, he fell with his face to the ground and prayed, "My Father, if it is possible, may this cup be taken from me. Yet not as I will, but as you will."

Then he returned to his disciples and found them sleeping. "Could you men not keep watch with me for one hour?" he asked Peter. "Watch and pray so that you will not fall into temptation. The spirit is willing, but the body is weak."

He went away a second time and prayed, "My Father, if it is not possible for this cup to be taken away unless I drink it, may your will be done."

When he came back, he again found them sleeping, because their eyes were heavy. So he left them and went away once more and prayed the third time, saying the same thing.

Then he returned to the disciples and said to them, "Are you still sleeping and resting? Look, the hour is near, and the Son of Man is betrayed into the hands of sinners. Rise, let us go! Here comes my betrayer!"

1. Contrast Jesus' prayer of absolute surrender to His Father with the poem below by Wilbur Rees:

I would like to buy three dollars worth of God, please.
Not enough to explode my soul or disturb my sleep,
but just enough to equal a cup of warm milk
or a snooze in the sunshine. . . .
I want ecstasy, not transformation;
I want the warmth of the womb, not a new birth.
I want a pound of the Eternal in a paper sack.
I would like to buy three dollars worth of God, please.

What stands out to you as the biggest difference between Jesus' prayer in Gethsemane and Wilbur Rees's poem?

....

....

....

....

2. On a scale from 1 to 10, which mindset are you closer to right now?

1	2	3	4	5	6	7	8	9	10

I'd settle for three dollars' worth of God

I want to surrender completely to God's will.

3. What areas of your life are you most reluctant to surrender to God? Why?

....

....

....

....

dig

A great way to deepen your understanding of Scripture is something that is called "inductive Bible study." This method of reading the Bible is a bit like being an investigative journalist. The goal is to set aside your assumptions and answer five basic questions: (1) Who? (2) What? (3) Where? (4) When? (5) Why? After you've answered those questions, you can figure out how the passage applies to your life (something you can't possibly know until you know the whole story, right?).

Look at the passage you read in Matthew 26:36-46 again. Now it's time to investigate the events of that night in Gethsemane and find out what it means for your mind and heart. If you are doing this study with a group, you can work with a partner—other believers are good sources for this kind of investigation.

1. **Who** are the persons involved in this passage?

2. **What** is taking place?

How many times did Jesus ask God to remove the cup?

What is the "cup"?

_____

_____

_____

_____

_____

_____

What is the prayer of relinquishment?

_____

_____

_____

_____

_____

3. **Where** is this event taking place?

_____

_____

_____

_____

_____

4. **When** does this event take place in Jesus' ministry on earth?

_____

_____

_____

_____

5. **Why** does Jesus pray the prayer of relinquishment?

_____

_____

_____

_____

_____

Does the prayer have consequences? If so, what are they?

_____

_____

_____

_____

_____

6. Now it's time to put all the information together to form a "big idea" that can be applied to your life. Jesus said, "Father, if you are willing, take this cup from me; yet not my will, but yours be done" (Luke 22:42). Theologian Richard Foster calls the prayer of relinquishment a prayer of self-emptying, surrender, abandonment, release and reservation.[1] Do you see these principles at work in Jesus' prayer? If so, how?

_____

_____

_____

_____

_____

7. Do you see these principles at work in your life? If so, in what areas?

8. In what areas of your life do you find these principles lacking?

9. How would your life look different if you were to pray the prayer of relinquishment?

apply

If there is a secret to living the Christian life, it is found through our obedience. Through our obedient life comes freedom and fulfillment.

1. Read John 14:21. If we say we love God, what will be the result?

_____

_____

_____

_____

2. Why is this an important principle for our lives?

_____

_____

_____

3. Read Philippians 2:5-11. According to these verses, what attitude did Jesus have?

_____

_____

_____

_____

4. What was the result of Jesus' obedience?

_____

_____

_____

_____

5. In what ways is your attitude similar to that of Jesus? How is it different?

6. What do you need to relinquish in order to be obedient?

reflect

Relinquishment is no easy task. Even Jesus struggled to release His will completely—He prayed the prayer three times, pouring sweat and blood! If you struggle with releasing your will to God, you are in good company:

- Abraham had to release his son Isaac (see Genesis 22).
- Moses had to release his will for the sake of Israel and Egypt (see Exodus 4; 7:1-6).
- David had to release his will for the son he had with Bath-sheba (see 2 Samuel 12:16-22).
- Paul had to release his desire to be free of his "thorn in the flesh" (see 2 Corinthians 12:7-10).

1. What part of your life is God calling you to give completely to Him through a prayer of relinquishment?

2. Read Galatians 2:20. How does this Scripture relate to the prayer of relinquishment?

3. Crucifixion is a slow, terribly gruesome way to die. Sometimes it can feel as though our old, sinful self is never going to just get it over with! What part of your old self is hanging on for all its worth, holding you back from total surrender to your new life in Christ?

4. You are called to become like Jesus: righteous, holy and surrendered to the Father. Don't settle for three dollars of God. When you are ready, write your prayer of relinquishment below.

meditation

Father, if you are willing, take this cup from me;
yet not my will, but yours be done.

LUKE 22:42

Note
1. Richard J. Foster, *Prayer: Finding the Heart's True Home* (San Francisco, CA: Harper Collins, 1992), pp. 47-56.

interceding
for others

My prayer is not for them alone. I pray also for those who will believe in me through their message, that all of them may be one, Father, just as you are in me and I am in you. May they also be in us so that the world may believe that you have sent me. I have given them the glory that you gave me, that they may be one as we are one: I in them and you in me. May they be brought to complete unity to let the world know that you sent me and have loved them even as you have loved me.

JOHN 17:20-23

The time set for Jesus' sacrifice on our behalf was approaching. He had so much to think about: the coming physical pain, unbearable humiliation, abandonment by everyone He loved. Yet somehow, He was able to set aside these foreboding thoughts and focus His attention on His followers, lifting them up to His Father in prayer.

Jesus set the standard for intercession; He brought others' needs before the Father's throne even when it was "inconvenient."

How many of us intercede as an afterthought, as a tag-on to our self-centered requests? Perhaps if we could gain a proper understanding of intercession, we would hit our knees more often.

Jesus' prayer for His followers (present and future) was a natural expression of His deep and abiding love. And this is how it must be for us: Our love for others sends us to the Father, the One who can heal their wounds, mend their hearts and fill them with His presence.

We must also learn to intercede for those who are difficult to love in our own power. It's been said there is nothing that makes us love a person so much as praying for him or her. Why? Because praying for someone invites God to open the eyes of our hearts to see that person as He sees them.

This is how the unity of Christ's Body is created! As we love one another, we pray for each other's needs. As those needs are met, each believer is strengthened and equipped to continue God's work of loving redemption and re-creation.

Are you praying for your family? For your church's other leaders? For the youth under your spiritual care? Are you praying for the difficult people in your life? Whether you begin with love and turn to pray, or begin with prayer and are turned to love, God is calling you to set aside your own distractions and circumstances to intercede for those around you.

True intercession involves bringing the person, or the circumstance that seems to be crashing in on you, before God, until you are changed by His attitude toward that person or circumstance. People describe intercession by saying, "It is putting yourself in someone else's place." That is not true! Intercession is putting yourself in God's place; it is having His mind and His perspective.
OSWALD CHAMBERS, *MY UTMOST FOR HIS HIGHEST*

interceding
for others

starter

EXPRESS IT! How do you express your love for others?

- ☐ I tell them.
- ☐ I assume they know.
- ☐ I write notes, emails or text messages.
- ☐ I try to do something nice for them.
- ☐ I help when they ask.
- ☐ I give hugs.
- ☐ I try not to say hurtful things.
- ☐ I spend time with them.
- ☐ Other _____

1. What is your favorite way for your family to express their love for you?

_____

_____

_____

_____

_____

2. What about your friends?

_____

_____

_____

_____

_____

message

The Gospel of John records something extraordinary: Jesus' prayer to the heavenly Father *for us*. That's right . . . Jesus prayed for everyone who would hear His disciples' message and believe in Him. As you read this prayer recorded in John 17:20-26, consider the following questions: (1) What is Jesus' prayer for us? (2) What is He asking the Father regarding unity among believers? (3) What does He ask for Himself?

My prayer is not for [my disciples] alone. I pray also for those who will believe in me through their message, that all of them may be one, Father, just as you are in me and I am in you. May they also be in us so that the world may believe that you have sent me. I have given them the glory that you gave me, that they may be one as we are one: I in them and you in me. May they be brought to complete unity to let the world know that you sent me and have loved them even as you have loved me. Father, I want those you have given me to be with me where I am, and to see my glory, the glory you have given me because you loved me before the creation of the world. Righteous Father, though the world does not know you, I know you, and they know that you have sent me. I have made you known to them, and will continue to make you known in order that the love you have for me may be in them and that I myself may be in them.

1. There are a couple of startling things about this prayer, not least of which is *when* Jesus prayed it. Take a look at the next chapter, John 18. When did Jesus offer His prayer to the Father on our behalf?

    ----

2. If you were about to be arrested, put on trial and then executed, would praying for others be high on your list of priorities? Why or why not?

    ----

3. What do you think the timing of Jesus' prayer says about His priorities?

4. How many times does the word "love" or "loved" appear in Jesus' prayer? Why do you think this is significant?

5. How are unity and love related?

6. Why do you think the unity of all believers was so important to Jesus?

7. How might praying for someone be an expression of your love for them?

_____

_____

_____

_____

8. It has been said that nothing makes us love someone more than praying for them. How do you think praying for a person who is difficult to love could change your attitude toward that person?

_____

_____

_____

_____

dig

Jesus asked the Father to help us love one another in unity. Many of the New Testament writers believed that praying for each other is an obvious part of loving one another. For instance, James wrote, "Is any one of you in trouble? He should pray. Is anyone happy? Let him sing songs of praise. Is any one of you sick? He should call the elders of the church to pray over him and anoint him with oil in the name of the Lord. And the prayer offered in faith will make the sick person well; the Lord will raise him up. If he has sinned, he will be forgiven. Therefore confess your sins to each other and pray for each other so that you may be healed. The prayer of a righteous man is powerful and effective" (James 5:13-16).

1. Have you ever prayed for someone who was sick and they got well? What happened?

2. Have you ever prayed for someone who was sick and they *didn't* get well? What happened?

3. What do you think was the difference?

4. What is "the prayer offered in faith"?

5. Have you ever prayed for someone who was spiritually, mentally or emotionally sick? How does that relate to this passage?

_____

_____

_____

_____

_____

6. How does praying for someone to be physically healed or spiritually restored express love?

_____

_____

_____

_____

_____

apply

1. Paul wrote this command to the church in Galatia: "Carry each other's burdens, and in this way you will fulfill the law of Christ" (Galatians 6:2). What do you think it means to "carry each other's burdens"?

_____

_____

_____

_____

2. Do you know someone who is struggling? How might you
    be able to share his or her load?

    _____

    _____

    _____

    _____

    _____

    _____

3. Do you think it is enough to pray for someone whom you
    might be able to help? How might you be God's answer to
    your prayer?

    _____

    _____

    _____

    _____

    _____

    _____

4. How do you think carrying each other's burdens relates to
    Jesus' prayer for love and unity? In what ways?

    _____

    _____

    _____

    _____

    _____

    _____

    _____

5. How often do you pray for your own needs before others' needs? How might your perspective change if you prayed for others first?

_____

_____

_____

_____

6. Who around you is hurting? Express your love for those people by writing out a prayer for them below.

_____

_____

_____

_____

_____

reflect

Part of following the command to carry each other's burdens is allowing others to help us. It can be difficult or embarrassing to ask others for help, but that doesn't let us off the hook.

1. Have you ever been sick (in body, heart or spirit) and asked for prayer? What happened?

_____

_____

_____

_____

2. Do you know of someone who prays for you regularly, such as a friend, parent, grandparent or youth leader? If so, how do you feel about it? If not, who will you ask to pray for you?

_____

_____

_____

_____

_____

_____

3. Do you need special prayer for a burden you are carrying? With whom will you share it?

_____

_____

_____

_____

_____

_____

4. How can letting others love us by praying for us create more unity?

_____

_____

_____

_____

_____

_____

5. Ask your friends and family what they need prayer for and make a list below. Share your needs with them, too. After a week, check in to see how God is answering your prayers and drawing you together in unity, just as Jesus prayed.

_____

_____

_____

_____

_____

_____

_____

_____

meditation

May they be brought to complete unity to let
the world know that you sent me and have loved them
even as you have loved me.

JOHN 17:23

does God always answer prayer?

But when you pray, go into your room, close the door and pray
to your Father, who is unseen. Then your Father,
who sees what is done in secret, will reward you.

MATTHEW 6:6

One author tells about his wonderful tropical fish aquarium. The man loved those fish; gazing into their world was a great visual respite for him when he wrote. The fish, however, were unaware of his love. In fact, when he interacted with the fish, they were terrified of him.

The fish also were prone to illness. When a fish became ill, the author had to remove it from the tank and medicate it until it was healthy again. This help, which was necessary to keep the fish alive, so terrified the sick fish that the shock alone could kill it. The author expressed his frustration that there was no way for him to communicate to the fish to tell them how much they meant to him, how much time he spent caring for them, or how he only wanted to help them. Unless the author could become a fish and tell them of his love, he wrote, they would never know about it.

We (the fish, so to speak) so often talk about answers to prayer as if we were grading God (our owner and keeper) on His performance. He either did or did not answer our prayer according to what we think He should have done. But let's pick up the line of this fish story, if you'll pardon the pun. Our judgmental responses to God's answers usually hinge on our mistrust of Him. That's not a pretty picture for people who sing heartily about faith in God and simply trusting every day. But it's not faith at all to trust Him when He has done what we've asked! Truly trusting Him happens when He doesn't seem to be answering what we view as an urgent need, when He says no to something we are certain we must have.

At that moment, true faith stops struggling and folds its hands. It recalls how much He loves us and reaffirms that He really does know what is best for us and that His love for us is far greater than even our love for ourselves. He proved His love completely when He came to earth—became a "fish"—and gave up His life. Paul puts it this way: "He who did not spare his own Son, but gave him up for us all—how will he not also, along with him, graciously give us all things?" (Romans 8:32). There is nothing we want that He won't give to us, if it's what is best for us. Trust Him. He is truly worthy of our trust!

We should have no doubt that our prayer is acceptable and heard,
and we must leave to God the measure, manner, time, and place,
for God will surely do what is right.
MARTIN LUTHER

does God always answer prayer?

starter

PRAYER SURVEY: Circle the number that best represents your position for each of the issues below. There are no correct answers in this survey. The idea is just to see where you stand on the various questions that come up regarding prayer.

1	2	3	4	5	6	7	8	9	10

I believe beyond a shadow of a doubt that God answers prayer.

I believe there is a God, but I question whether He is interested in what I do.

1	2	3	4	5	6	7	8	9	10

I don't always know how
God answers prayers, but I
always have faith He will.

When I fail to see an
obvious answer, I wonder
if God answers at all.

1	2	3	4	5	6	7	8	9	10

I often praise and thank
God as well as ask
Him for things.

I treat God a lot like
Santa Claus. Give me
this; give me that.

1	2	3	4	5	6	7	8	9	10

When God says no,
I feel it is for my own good.

It's hard for me to
accept an answer of "no."

1	2	3	4	5	6	7	8	9	10

When God answers a prayer,
my faith is strengthened.

I think that answered
prayer is just a coincidence.

1	2	3	4	5	6	7	8	9	10

When God says, "Wait
awhile," I accept His timing
without reservation.

I prayed once and God
never answered, so I don't
pray much anymore.

1	2	3	4	5	6	7	8	9	10

I find myself praying
throughout the day.

Days go by
and I never pray.

1	2	3	4	5	6	7	8	9	10

When I don't feel like praying
is when I pray the hardest.

When I don't feel like
praying, I don't pray at all.

1	2	3	4	5	6	7	8	9	10

I feel as comfortable praying in public as I do alone.   I don't feel comfortable praying in public.

1	2	3	4	5	6	7	8	9	10

I feel that my prayer life is really growing.   I have almost buried my prayer life.

message

When you ask a parent or other adult in authority for something, do they always say yes? If so, you are in a tiny minority! Adults who care about you sometimes answer no to your requests. They give you an answer, even if it's not always the answer you want.

When we ask God for something in prayer, He always answers. Sometimes His answer is *go*. He gives the go-ahead and grants our request. Sometimes His answer is *no*. We ask, but He sees a bigger picture and refuses our request. Perhaps what we've asked for is not what is best for us. Other times, God's answer is *grow*. The answer will eventually be yes, but we've got some growing and trusting to do first; the time isn't yet right. He always answers prayer, even if it's not always the answer we want.

1. Read the Scriptures below and decide what God's answer was for each prayer—go, no or grow—and then write why you think that was His answer. Don't forget to practice inductive Bible study to figure out what's really going on (see the previous session for inductive study guidelines).

But Abram said, "O Sovereign Lord, what can you give me since I remain childless and the one who will inherit my estate is Eliezer

*of Damascus?" And Abram said, "You have given me no children;
so a servant in my household will be my heir." Then the word of
the* LORD *came to him: "This man will not be your heir, but a son
coming from your own body will be your heir." He took him outside and said, "Look up at the heavens and count the stars—if indeed you can count them." Then he said to him, "So shall your
offspring be"* (Genesis 15:2-5).

Go, **no** or **grow**?

Why?

_____

_____

_____

_____

*Father, if you are willing, take this cup from me; yet not my will,
but yours be done* (Luke 22:42).

Go, **no** or **grow**?

Why?

_____

_____

_____

_____

One day Peter and John were going up to the temple at the time of prayer—at three in the afternoon. Now a man crippled from birth was being carried to the temple gate called Beautiful, where he was put every day to beg from those going into the temple courts. When he saw Peter and John about to enter, he asked them for money. Peter looked straight at him, as did John. Then Peter said, "Look at us!" So the man gave them his attention, expecting to get something from them.

Then Peter said, "Silver or gold I do not have, but what I have I give you. In the name of Jesus Christ of Nazareth, walk." Taking him by the right hand, he helped him up, and instantly the man's feet and ankles became strong. He jumped to his feet and began to walk. Then he went with them into the temple courts, walking and jumping, and praising God. When all the people saw him walking and praising God, they recognized him as the same man who used to sit begging at the temple gate called Beautiful, and they were filled with wonder and amazement at what had happened to him (Acts 3:1-20).

Go, **no** or **grow**?

Why?

2. When has God answered one of your requests with *go, no* or *grow*? Describe each situation below.

Go:

_____

_____

_____

_____

_____

_____

No:

_____

_____

_____

_____

_____

_____

Grow:

_____

_____

_____

_____

_____

dig

A 17-year-old girl died after a "faith healer" prayed for her healing and her parents pulled the plug. Against the wishes of the medical staff in the hospital, the parents of 17-year-old Debra Barker stopped her hospital respirator because they believed she was healed. Debra Barker had been in a coma for three days after a tragic accident in which she was thrown from her car. Evidence showed the passengers of the car had been drinking.

Pastor Stephen Johnson of Community Church said that Debra's parents asked Reverend Jesse Thomas, a faith healer who had just preached at the church, to come to the hospital to pray for their daughter. Reverend Thomas, Pastor Johnson and Debra's parents entered the hospital room at approximately 1:00 in the afternoon. After Reverend Thomas prayed for Debra, he said she was healed as he felt warmth flow through his hands onto her forehead. Debra's parents, "in faith," pulled the plug to the respirator without the permission of the hospital staff. Debra died 12 minutes later.

1. What do you think about Reverend Thomas?

2. What do you think about Debra's parents?

3. What is the role of faith when it comes to prayer?

4. Why didn't God heal Debra?

5. What lesson or idea can you take away from this story?

6. How does it relate to your prayer life?

apply

1. Read James 4:2. Imagine a wealthy family with a 10-year-old son. Come up with a scenario that might happen in that family to demonstrate this verse.

    _____

    _____

    _____

    _____

    _____

    _____

    _____

2. Now read James 4:3. Continue your scenario—what happens next?

    _____

    _____

    _____

    _____

    _____

    _____

3. Read Matthew 6:5-7. What is the reward for those who are "prayer show-offs"?

    _____

    _____

    _____

    _____

    _____

4. Why do you think God is more likely to answer *no* when we show off?

_____

_____

_____

_____

_____

5. Why do you think God is more likely to answer *go* or *grow* when we are humble?

_____

_____

_____

_____

_____

6. Is it possible to pray in a group without showing off? What are some ways you can avoid falling into the "hypocrite trap"?

_____

_____

_____

_____

_____

7. What makes an answer of *go* or *grow* so difficult to handle?

_____

_____

_____

_____

8. Why is *no* so often a very good answer to prayer?

_____

_____

_____

_____

_____

_____

9. Where have you seen God's love and care in your life when He gave you an answer you weren't looking for?

_____

_____

_____

_____

_____

reflect

The Serenity Prayer was written by theologian Reinhold Niebuhr for use in one of his sermons back in 1934. The prayer was first circulated by the Federal Council of Churches and later by the U.S. armed forces. Eventually, it was adopted by 12-step programs, such as Alcoholics Anonymous, around the world. Members say it together at every meeting. It goes like this:

God, grant me the serenity
to accept the things I cannot change;
the courage to accept the things I can;
and the wisdom to know the difference.

1. How does the Serenity Prayer relate to God's three possible answers (*go, no* or *grow*)?

2. How might praying the Serenity Prayer impact your spiritual life?

3. For what do you need serenity? For what do you need courage?

4. Write a short prayer for those situations now. If you like,
    share your requests with a friend or your group so that
    you can pray for each other.

---

meditation

But when you pray, go into your room, close the door and
pray to your Father, who is unseen. Then your Father,
who sees what is done in secret, will reward you.

MATTHEW 6:6

unit III

developing a disciplined devotional life

I've told students for years that a disciplined devotional life with God is not an option but a necessity for spiritual growth. However, for most of my years of youth ministry it was one of the greatest struggles of my life. I tried every devotional program ever written and failed miserably at all of them. I think I kept waiting for "the feeling," whatever that means.

Then one day in the quietness of my bedroom, I got on my knees before God and I said something like, "Lord, I'm ashamed of what little time I spend with You." I almost expected a lightning bolt to come out of heaven and zap me. Out of my lack of discipline and my desire to grow in my relationship with God, I started to say, "Lord, I will commit two hours a day of devotional time with You."

A friend of mine in seminary told me Billy Graham gave God a tenth of his day. However, I knew that wouldn't last, so I started to say, "God, I will give You one hour every day for the rest of my life." *If my friend Becky can do that then I surely can do the same*, I thought. Again, I knew I was opting for failure. Half an hour? Nope.

"Okay, God, I'll give you 20 minutes a day for the rest of my life." I half expected a "what a spiritual wimp" to come from the voice of God, but instead I sensed a real peace. That commitment was in 1985. I've missed a few days, but not many. I can't always remember what I read or prayed about—but then, I can't tell you what I ate last week, although the food nourishes me today.

Paul's advice to Timothy was "train yourself to be godly" (1 Timothy 4:7). Our job in this section is not to pour on heaps of guilt and try to shame our students into a devotional life. We know in our hearts that that won't work. Our goal is to give our students every opportunity to listen to the Word of God and develop a practical devotional life that works for them.

Christian psychologists tell us that it only takes three weeks to form a habit and another three weeks to solidify that habit for life. We tend to talk in church about bad habits more often than good habits. Yet developing a daily time with God is a great habit. You have the privilege in these next few sessions to provide an "apple of gold" for your students. As you guide them into developing a regular time of communication and devotion to God, you will help your young people change their spiritual lives forever. (Who says youth work isn't important!)

Caution: These next few sessions may cause an eternal difference in the lives of your students. Thanks again for your availability to be a difference-maker in the lives of your students. God bless you!

be a disciplined disciple

Very early in the morning, while it was still dark, Jesus got up, left the house and went off to a solitary place, where he prayed.

MARK 1:35

There once was a boy who lived in his father's home where his dad took care to provide him with everything he needed. The father also gave his son many other things, just to show his love.

But the boy seldom returned his father's displays of affection. He rarely talked to his father at all, for there were so many other things to do—so many other ways to spend his time than with his dad. He accepted his dad's gifts; sometimes when he used them, he offered a brief "Thank you" in passing. But time spent in building a relationship with Dad wasn't a priority.

The boy really didn't know his father as a person. Dad was just the provider of resources. The son really didn't know what his dad was like—what made him happy or the things he cared about. In a sense, he was his father's son in name only.

Does this sound like your average "ungrateful child"? Or does it sound more like you and me? Yes, we are related to our Father and are living in His house of grace. He goes above and beyond the call of duty to prove His love for us. He constantly calls our names, makes efforts to bring us close to Him. But are we His children in name only?

Until we carve out time and make regular opportunities to get to know our Father for who He is, to begin to appreciate Him for Himself, we remain at the level of self-absorbed children who are His in name only. It's not enough to be thankful in passing for the gifts but rarely stop to get intimate with the Giver. And as we have already seen, intimacy with God is what changes us and grows us into people who *know* Him, not people who know *about* Him. He is not looking for a legalistic, hours-long commitment to some religious form: He wants *you*. And there is no sweeter, more valuable time in life this side of heaven—no matter what the tyranny of the urgent seems to scream at us.

Crises will always be there. But to give God the best of ourselves in a new day, to spend time talking with Him at night, is a discipline that will soon grow to a hunger for His presence—if we lay down our preconceived notions of what we have to *do* and let our Father guide us into intimate relationship with Him. Grow beyond being His child in name only!

A spiritual life without discipline is impossible.
Discipline is the other side of discipleship.
HENRI NOUWEN

be a disciplined disciple

starter

YOUR CHOICE: "Disciple" is not a word most people put on their top-10 favorites list. It just doesn't have the same ring as "spontaneity" or "free-spiritedness."

1. If you could develop any talent, what would it be? Why?

_____

_____

_____

_____

_____

_____

2. If you had to choose between sleeping in on Saturday morning or getting up early to do something difficult yet rewarding (youth group fundraiser? sports tournament? SAT prep?), which would you choose? Why?

    _____

    _____

    _____

    _____

    _____

    _____

3. Which phrase best describes you?

    ☐   Totally disciplined to the point of boring
    ☐   More disciplined than most
    ☐   Sometimes disciplined, other times not
    ☐   Spontaneous most of the time
    ☐   Flaky

4. In what areas of your life would you like to be more disciplined? In what areas would you like to be more spontaneous?

    More disciplined:

    _____

    _____

    _____

    _____

More spontaneous:

_____

_____

_____

_____

message

A disciplined daily devotional life is not optional for spiritual growth; it's a must! If we desire to grow closer to God and into spiritual maturity, we must pray, study Scripture and fellowship with other Christians regularly. These are the foundational disciplines for spiritual growth.

1. How would you rate your devotional life right now?

    ☐   Hoping to get started
    ☐   Up and down
    ☐   Boring
    ☐   Getting better
    ☐   Going strong
    ☐   What devotional life?
    ☐   Other _____

2. Which of the three foundational disciplines is your strongest area? Which is your weakest?

    _____

    _____

    _____

    _____

3. Imagine opening your mailbox and finding an envelope addressed to you. The return address says, "God." Here's what's inside:

My Dear Child,

I love you. I desire to spend as much time with you as possible. I took great joy in being part of your creation and your salvation. I consider My sacrifice for you a sign of My significant love for you. My child, I want the best for you. I believe in you. I look forward to our daily times together. It gives Me great pleasure to spend time with you. Don't forget, I'm always with you.

Love, God

How would you feel if you received this letter?

_____

_____

_____

_____

4. What decisions would you want to make about your time with God?

_____

_____

_____

_____

_____

5. It has been estimated that the average person spends more than two hours a day watching television, two hours a day online, one hour a day dressing and grooming, and one hour a day eating. Yet the majority of people spend little or no time each day with God. A wise pastor once asked, "What is so important that you can't spend 15 minutes a day with God?" What's your answer?

....

....

....

....

6. What makes it difficult to set up a daily time with God?

....

....

....

....

dig

Developing a regular and rich devotional life is difficult for many people because they don't know how. Having a pattern or structure can help them get in the habit of meeting with God every day. Read about the following elements of an effective devotional life as you enjoy some time with God.

Bible reading

God's Word is His revelation to us about who He is and who He wants us to be. If you truly want to get to know Him, there is no better place to start. There are tons and tons of Bible study resources available to guide you if you're not sure how to get started reading Scripture; ask your youth leader for some recommendations. Alternately, you might want to begin with one of the four Gospels (Matthew, Mark, Luke or John) to learn all you can about Jesus.

A good tool for studying Scripture is inductive Bible study, which is explored in session 6 of this book. When you study the Bible inductively, you ask *who? what? where? when? why?* to get to the heart of a particular passage. Try it with the verses below, on your own or with a friend or group. (Tip: Read the entire chapter where the verses are found. You may also want to reference a concordance or study Bible.)

"All men are like grass, and all their glory is like the flowers of the field; the grass withers and the flowers fall, but the word of the Lord stands forever." And this is the word that was preached to you (1 Peter 1:24-25).

1. **Who** are the persons involved in this passage?

_____

_____

_____

Who wrote this passage?

_____

_____

_____

2. **What** was happening to cause Peter to write these words?

_____

_____

_____

_____

What does Peter say men (and women) are like? What is their glory like?

_____

_____

_____

How long does the word of the Lord last?

_____

_____

_____

_____

3. **Where** were the believers to whom Peter was writing?

_____

_____

_____

_____

4. **When** was Peter writing this letter?

    ....

    ....

    ....

    ....

5. **Why** did Peter remind his readers about the word of the
    Lord?

    ....

    ....

    ....

    ....

    Why is it important for believers to know that the word of
    the Lord stands forever?

    ....

    ....

    ....

    ....

listening

Once you have read and studied a portion of God's Word, it is
time to meditate on the passage, allowing the Holy Spirit to
speak to you through those verses. Proverbs 2:1-2,5 says, "My son,
if you accept my words and store up my commands within you,
turning your ear to wisdom and applying your heart to understanding, then you will understand the fear of the LORD and find
the knowledge of God."

Slowly read the verses from 1 Peter again, thinking about the inductive study questions you answered about the passage. With all you have just learned about Peter's words to the early Christians, how is the Holy Spirit leading you to apply these verses to your life?

_____

_____

_____

_____

_____

prayer

Earlier, we discussed some the various components of prayer, including praise and thanksgiving, confession, and asking and listening. Now it's time to put each of these into practice.

1. *Praise and Thanksgiving.* "Let everything that has breath praise the LORD. Praise the LORD" (Psalm 150:6). Take a few minutes to tell God of His greatness and His majestic power. Adore Him for who He is: the Lord of lords and the King of kings. Then thank Him for specific things He has done in your life, in your family, in your church and in your friends' lives.

   Praise:

   _____

   _____

   _____

Thanksgiving:

_____

_____

_____

_____

_____

_____

2. *Confession.* "If we confess ours sins, he is faithful and just and will forgive us our sins and purify us from all unrighteousness" (1 John 1:9). We keep the communication lines open when we confess our sins to God. Take one minute to sit quietly before the Lord. When the Holy Spirit convicts you of sin, confess it to God. Don't forget to thank Him for His forgiveness.

_____

_____

_____

_____

_____

_____

3. *Asking and Listening.* "Ask and it will be given to you; seek and you will find; knock and the door will be opened to you" (Matthew 7:7). Take a few minutes to ask God for specific prayer requests. Pray for your family, church, school, friends, the government and yourself. Spend another minute or so in silence, inviting the Holy Spirit to speak to your heart.

Asking:

_____

_____

_____

_____

_____

Listening:

_____

_____

_____

_____

_____

apply

1. Why do you think it is difficult for many people to have a consistent time with God?

    _____

    _____

    _____

    _____

    _____

2. Name at least three ways a disciplined quiet time can bring you closer to God.

    _____

    _____

    _____

    _____

    _____

3. When is the best time of the day for you to take a few moments to be with the Lord? What other commitments need to be shifted around to make it happen?

    _____

    _____

    _____

    _____

    _____

4. How can you integrate your own creativity into your times with God?

    _____

    _____

    _____

    _____

    _____

reflect

Now that you have had a guided devotional time as part of this session, what keeps you from doing it on a daily basis? If you are ready to make a commitment to a disciplined devotional life, fill in the appointment card below.

---

a daily appointment with God

What time? _____

How long? _____

Where? _____

What to bring: _____

Consider sharing your appointment card with a friend who will keep you accountable to your commitment. (Fellowship with other Christians is important too, so don't do it all on your own!)

meditation

Very early in the morning, while it was still dark,
Jesus got up, left the house and went off to a
solitary place, where he prayed.

MARK 1:35

worship

> *Come, let us bow down in worship, let us kneel*
> *before the LORD our Maker.*
> PSALM 95:6

What image does the word "worship" call into your mind? Tall stained-glass windows, organ music, choirs robed and harmonious? Soaring, epic guitars and hands raised to the heavens? The majesty of a quiet, distant mountain cathedral, the glory of a beautiful forest? Where do you worship?

Perhaps like the disobedient Israelites, who made high places from which to worship God, it's easier to give priority to place and form than it is to understand worship in spirit and truth. But inside we know that worship is not a place. Nor is worship about form, the ways we express our love to God. It's not about church meetings—even though it's wonderful to worship as a family with our brothers and sisters—because even in church, there can only be corporate worship at the level of what the individual worshipers bring. If we aren't worshiping God every day, we have nothing to bring with which to worship when the Body meets!

So what is worship? It is, as Jesus said, a matter of spirit and truth. It's what is going on in your heart *before* anything reaches your lips. First, it's that daily time to stop and appreciate God, time taken both in a block, when we focus on Him, and in little moments, when we pause to give Him the honor and reverence that are His due. It's being with Him, in awareness and attention, talking to Him, listening to Him and telling ourselves (and whoever else is listening) that God alone is worthy of all our praise. Worship can happen on a city street or even in a humble bathroom. It's not place; it's not form. It's a spirit full of praise and a mind growing in the truth of God's Word. It's the sacrifice we are required to make (see Hebrews 13:15), the sacrifice that is delightful to bring to the One who is so very worthy of our worship!

You are the Fountain of Life, the Treasure of everlasting goods
to whom the heavens sing praise—all the angels and heavenly powers,
crying out to one another—while we, the weak and unworthy
join with them in singing: "Holy, holy, holy, Lord of God of Hosts,
the whole earth is full of your glory."
LANCELOT ANDREWS

group study guide

worship

starter

EXCUSES, EXCUSES: What are the 20 most common excuses you've made or heard for not coming to church? List as many as you can think of below. Be creative!

1. ....

2. ....

3. ....

4. ....

5. ....

6. ....

7. ....

8. _____

9. _____

10. _____

11. _____

12. _____

13. _____

14. _____

15. _____

16. _____

17. _____

18. _____

19. _____

20. _____

Out of those 20, which three are the most ridiculous?

1. _____

2. _____

3. _____

message

For each of the following words, write down the first thing that comes to mind. Don't think too hard about your answers; just write whatever pops in your head. When you've done that for each word, go back and write why you think you responded in that way. Discuss your answers with a friend or group.

Sermon: _____

Why? _____

_____

_____

_____

Sacraments: _____

Why? _____

_____

_____

_____

Offering: _____

Why? _____

_____

_____

Praying Together: _____

Why? _____

_____

_____

_____

Time with God: _____

Why? _____

_____

_____

_____

Worship Music: _____

Why? _____

_____

_____

_____

It may sound strange, but worship is not about any of these things. We use these various methods—worship music, offerings, sacraments—to express our worship to God, but they are not, in and of themselves, worship. Jesus said, "A time is coming and has now come when the true worshipers will worship the Father in spirit and truth, for they are the kind of worshipers the Father seeks" (John 4:23). Worship is, first, a matter of spirit. The ways we worship God are a reflection of what is in our hearts.

1. Read Psalm 122. What is the attitude of the person speaking in verse 1?

_____

_____

_____

2. A great philosopher once said, "When it comes to worship, we should never ask 'How was it?' We should ask 'How did I do?'" How is this statement different from what most people think of when it comes to worship?

_____

_____

_____

_____

_____

_____

3. To participate in and enjoy a good worship experience, we must develop a proper attitude and a proper spirit. How do you prepare to worship?

_____

_____

_____

_____

_____

_____

4. What are a few specific things you can do to understand and enjoy your worship experience?

_____

_____

_____

_____

_____

dig

1. According to Psalm 122:3-4, why did the tribes of the Lord come to Jerusalem?

2. Read Psalm 100. How would you describe your feelings after reading that passage?

3. Can you describe the relationship between worship and praise? What's the difference?

4. According to verse 5, what is the best reason to offer God our praise?

5. Look again at Psalm 122. In verses 6-8, what does the writer pray for? Answer in your own words—how might you pray for peace in our day and age?

_____

_____

_____

_____

6. How is time spent with God in prayer a form of worship?

_____

_____

_____

_____

apply

God deserves our praise; that is reason enough to worship. Yet there are also amazing benefits *we* receive when we cultivate an attitude and a habit of worship—and the very best of these blessings is *peace*.

1. Read John 14:27. What do you think Jesus meant by the word "peace"?

_____

_____

_____

_____

2. Take a "peace inventory." Next to each area of your life, place an X under the phrase that best describes how peaceful you are.

	Total Peace	Some Peace	No Peace at all
Relationship with God	☐	☐	☐
Family life	☐	☐	☐
Friendships	☐	☐	☐
School	☐	☐	☐
Your future	☐	☐	☐
How you feel about yourself	☐	☐	☐

3. How might worshiping God increase your peace in each of these areas?

_____

_____

_____

_____

_____

4. Do you think a habit of worship could help you put your problems and challenges in perspective? Why or why not?

_____

_____

_____

_____

_____

5. What activity in your church's worship service is your favorite?

_____

_____

_____

_____

_____

6. What about in your personal worship time?

_____

_____

_____

_____

_____

7. Do you see a connection between your favorite worship activity and the level of peace you experience as a result? If so, in what way?

_____

_____

_____

_____

_____

reflect

There are two types of worship: *corporate* and *personal*. Corporate worship is done with other believers, and personal worship is, of course, one's own time with God. Both aspects of worship are essential to a good relationship with God.

1. Check the word that best describes your level of participation in each of the following four elements of *personal* worship. Make goals to improve those areas that need work.

Level of Participation

	Major	Some	Not Much	None
Praise	☐	☐	☐	☐
Bible Study	☐	☐	☐	☐
Prayer	☐	☐	☐	☐
Music	☐	☐	☐	☐

Praise goals:

_____

_____

Bible study goals:

_____

_____

Prayer goals:

_____

_____

Music goals:

_____

_____

2. Check the word that best describes your level of participation in each of the following six elements of *corporate* worship. Make goals to improve those areas that need work.

Level of Participation

	Major	Some	Not Much	None
Praise	☐	☐	☐	☐
Sermon	☐	☐	☐	☐
Prayer	☐	☐	☐	☐
Music	☐	☐	☐	☐
Giving	☐	☐	☐	☐
The Sacraments	☐	☐	☐	☐

Praise goals:

_____

_____

_____

Sermon goals:

_____

_____

_____

Prayer goals:

_____

_____

_____

Music goals:

_____

_____

_____

Giving goals:

The Sacraments goals:

meditation

Come, let us bow down in worship, let us kneel
before the Lord our Maker.

PSALM 95:6

the Bible

Do not let this Book of the Law depart from your mouth;
meditate on it day and night, so that you may be careful to do everything
written in it. Then you will be prosperous and successful.

JOSHUA 1:8

The next time you are casually paging through a food magazine, look at the adjectives used by those who write. They express a kind of boundless enthusiasm as they describe their food experiences: "Blissful . . . great . . . pleasing . . . perfect . . . best . . . particularly good . . . favorite . . . fine . . . ample . . . superb . . ." The list could go on and on. Enthusiastic adjectives abound! There is no doubt, as one reads the words of those who have tasted, that what they are describing is wonderful! It sounds like the best stuff on earth!

Which of those adjectives describes what you tasted today as you sat down to your portion of God's Amazing Meal? Was it a *blissful* time, full of *great* truth and *pleasing* understanding? (Even a non-pleasing new understanding can be good for us!) We already know that God's method for filling our souls and growing our spirits in Him is the *best* food source available. It's *particularly good* when we are famished for something more than the world can offer us, when we are hungry and thirsty for some reality in the midst of a world run amuck, a world where whole publications are given over to delighting the palate and worshiping the stomach!

We could play with the adjectives some more, but you get the point. What did God feed you today? Are you appreciating it, blissfully chewing it slowly so as to reap the full benefit of what He has for you? Are you digesting it, making it part of you in every way, asking the Holy Spirit to show you how to apply God's truth in the smallest details of your life? His Word is the finest, most nourishing food available. And you can have all you want! There are no calories—but the energy available through it is staggering. Don't skip this meal in favor of any of the world's junk-food substitutes. When it comes to your spiritual life, take the best that God wants to give you and eat!

To receive any deep, inward profit from the Scripture
you must read as I have described. Plunge into the very depths
of the words you read until revelation, like a sweet
aroma, breaks out upon you.

JEANNE GUYON

the Bible

starter

THE RULES: Are there times when you're more or less likely to follow directions? Place an *X* beside each situation to indicate the likelihood of you following the rules.

	More Likely	Less Likely
Putting together a new bike.	❏	❏
My parents tell me to clean the house.	❏	❏
A teacher gives me a special homework assignment.	❏	❏
The Bible tells me what to do with my life.	❏	❏
I'm driving on the highway and no one is looking.	❏	❏

1. What are your reasons for following directions in the situations when you're more likely to follow the rules?

   ....
   ....
   ....
   ....

2. What are your reasons for *not* following directions in the situations when you're less likely to follow the rules?

   ....
   ....
   ....
   ....

message

When you don't follow the rules, there can be unfortunate consequences. For each scriptural command below, list three possible results of not knowing or not living out the Bible's instructions.

"Love your neighbor as yourself" (Galatians 5:14).

1. ....
   ....
   ....

2. ....
   ....

3.

"Honor your father and your mother" (Exodus 20:12).

1.

2.

3.

"Avoid sexual immorality" (1 Thessalonians 4:3).

1.

2.

3.

dig

While the Bible has some pretty straightforward guidelines for God's people to follow, it's much more than a rulebook. But what exactly is it? Here are a few questions to answer individually, with a partner or in a group that will help you get to know your Bible.

1. How many books are in the Bible? _____

2. How many books are in the Old Testament (sometimes called the Hebrew Bible)? _____

3. How many books are in the New Testament? _____

4. In what language was most of the Old Testament originally written? _____

5. In what language was the New Testament originally written? _____

6. The Old Testament is divided into four parts. Name them.

    1. _____
    2. _____
    3. _____
    4. _____

7. The New Testament is divided into four parts. Name them.

    1. _____
    2. _____
    3. _____
    4. _____

8. What was the language that Jesus most likely spoke during His earthly ministry? _____

apply

As anyone who has a friend knows, *knowing about* someone is not the same as *knowing* that person. It's the same with God's Word. Knowing facts about the Bible is good, but it's nowhere near as important as knowing the Word of God and hiding it in our hearts, letting it change us from the inside out. Read the following Scriptures, and then answer the questions that follow.

> *Do not let this Book of the Law depart from your mouth; meditate on it day and night, so that you may be careful to do everything written in it. Then you will be prosperous and successful* (Joshua 1:8).

> *Blessed is the man who does not walk in the counsel of the wicked or stand in the way of sinners or sit in the seat of mockers. But his delight is in the law of the LORD, and on his law he meditates day and night. He is like a tree planted by streams of water, which yields its fruit in season and whose leaf does not wither. Whatever he does prospers. Not so the wicked! They are like chaff that the wind blows away. Therefore the wicked will not stand in the judgment, nor sinners in the assembly of the righteous. For the LORD watches over the way of the righteous, but the way of the wicked will perish* (Psalm 1).

1. According to Joshua 1:8 and Psalm 1, what are the benefits of meditating on (thinking about) God's Word?

_____

_____

_____

2. These Scriptures are not saying that problems will never come our way. But they do seem to say that those who continually place the Word of God in their hearts will have lives that are enriched by fulfillment and meaning. Throughout Scripture, God promises blessings to those who integrate His Word into their lives. These blessings include:

    - peace   - help to overcome sin
    - joy   - direction in life
    - truth

    Read each Scripture below, and then write the word from the list above that best describes the result of following God's Word.

    Psalm 119:11: _____

    Psalm 119:105: _____

    John 8:31-36: _____

    John 15:11: _____

    John 16:33: _____

    John 17:17: _____

3. For a better understanding of why we should read the Bible, take a look at 2 Timothy 3:16-17. What does it say about Scripture?

    _____

    _____

    _____

4. What is Scripture useful for?

_____

_____

_____

_____

_____

5. How can you see Scripture affecting your life in each of these ways?

_____

_____

_____

_____

_____

To know the Word and to live by it, you will need to take daily time to read the Bible. To develop a habit of Bible reading, it is best to have a consistent time and place. When and where will you take time to put God's Word to work in your life? You'll need a method. How will you begin? Here are three suggestions:

1. *A Month of Praise and Wisdom.* By reading less than 10 minutes a day for one month, you can go through the books of Psalms and Proverbs. The psalms are the beautiful songs of the Hebrew people, and the proverbs contain great, practical advice on many aspects of life. All you need to do is read five psalms and one proverb each day, and after a month you will have completed two of the greatest books in the Bible. Then you will be ready for a new plan and you will already have started the positive habit of reading the Bible each day.

2. *The 90-Day Experience.* Try an experiment that will change your life! You can read the entire New Testament in less than three months if you'll take 15 minutes a day, reading approximately 3 chapters per day. Listed is a format you can use to try this experiment. You'll be excited to see the positive results of incorporating biblical principles into your life.[1]

1. Matthew 1–4
2. Matthew 5–7
3. Matthew 8–10
4. Matthew 11–13
5. Matthew 14–16
6. Matthew 17–19
7. Matthew 20–22
8. Matthew 23–25
9. Matthew 26–28
10. Mark 1–3
11. Mark 4–6
12. Mark 7–9
13. Mark 10–12
14. Mark 13–16
15. Luke 1–3
16. Luke 4–6
17. Luke 7–9
18. Luke 10–12
19. Luke 13–15
20. Luke 16–18
21. Luke 19–21
22. Luke 22–24
23. John 1–3
24. John 4–6
25. John 7–9
26. John 10–12
27. John 13–16:4
28. John 16:5–18
29. John 19–21
30. Acts 1–3
31. Acts 4–6
32. Acts 7–9
33. Acts 10–12
34. Acts 13–15
35. Acts 16–18
36. Acts 19–21:36
37. Acts 21:37–25:22
38. Acts 25:23–28:30
39. Romans 1–3
40. Romans 4–6
41. Romans 7–8
42. Romans 9–11
43. Romans 12–13
44. Romans 14–16
45. 1 Corinthians 1–4
46. 1 Corinthians 5–7

47. 1 Corinthians 8–11
48. 1 Corinthians 12–14
49. 1 Corinthians 15–16
50. 2 Corinthians 1–3
51. 2 Corinthians 4–6
52. 2 Corinthians 7–9
53. 2 Corinthians 1–13
54. Galatians 1–2
55. Galatians 3–4
56. Galatians 5–6
57. Ephesians 1–3
58. Ephesians 4–6
59. Philippians 1–2
60. Philippians 3–4
61. Colossians 1–2
62. Colossians 3–4
63. 1 Thessalonians 1–3
64. 1 Thessalonians 4–5
65. 2 Thessalonians 1–3
66. 1 Timothy 1–3
67. 1 Timothy 4–6
68. 2 Timothy 1–4
69. Titus 1–3
70. Philemon
71. Hebrews 1–2
72. Hebrews 3–4:13
73. Hebrews 4:14–7
74. Hebrews 8–10
75. Hebrews 11–13
76. James 1–3:12
77. James 3:13–5
78. 1 Peter 1–3:7
79. 1 Peter 3:8–5
80. 2 Peter 1–3
81. 1 John 1–3:10
82. 1 John 3:11–5
83. 2 John; 3 John; Jude
84. Revelation 1–3
85. Revelation 4–6
86. Revelation 7–9
87. Revelation 10–12
88. Revelation 13–15
89. Revelation 16–18
90. Revelation 19–22

3. *Devotional Books:* Devotional books are written to plant the Word of God in your life and give you practical insight in your walk with God. In just 10 to 15 minutes a day, you can complete a devotional reading. Usually a devotional book has a Scripture, a story and a challenge or action steps for each day. Talk with your youth leader or other adult about some recommendations for devotional resources.

reflect

1. Some people have estimated that there are more than 3,000 promises in the Bible. Many of those promises are related to the area of prayer. Read each Scripture below, and then write out its promise and how it affects your life.

The promise in Isaiah 26:3:

_____

_____

_____

_____

How it affects my life:

_____

_____

_____

_____

The promise in Isaiah 40:31:

_____

_____

_____

How it affects my life:

_____

_____

_____

The promise in Jeremiah 33:3:

_____

_____

_____

_____

How it affects my life:

_____

_____

_____

The promise in Matthew 6:33:

_____

_____

_____

How it affects my life:

_____

_____

_____

_____

The promise in John 14:14:

_____

_____

_____

_____

How it affects my life:

_____

_____

_____

_____

_____

The promise in Philippians 4:6-7:

_____

_____

_____

_____

How it affects my life:

_____

_____

_____

_____

The promise in Philippians 4:19:

_____

_____

_____

How it affects my life:

_____

_____

_____

_____

The promise in 1 John 5:14-15:

_____

_____

_____

_____

How it affects my life:

_____

_____

_____

_____

2. What are the advantages of reading the Bible daily?

_____

_____

_____

_____

3. Why do you think God has given us the Bible to read?

_____

_____

_____

_____

4. What keeps you from spending more time in God's Word?

_____

_____

_____

_____

5. What specific steps will you take in the coming week to begin a daily habit of Bible study?

_____

_____

_____

_____

_____

_____

meditation

Do not let this Book of the Law depart from
your mouth; meditate on it day and night, so that you may
be careful to do everything written in it. Then you will be
prosperous and successful.

JOSHUA 1:8

Note

1. Jim Burns, *90 Days Through the New Testament* (Ventura, CA: Regal Books, 1990), pp. 15-135. Used by permission.

session 12

getting your spiritual life in shape

In a race all the runners run, but only one gets the prize. . . .
Run in such a way as to get the prize.
1 CORINTHIANS 9:24-27

We've all done it. When we notice that our clothes no longer fit or the bathroom scale is about to reach maximum capacity, we decide that we will *do* something! We buy exercise machines or new jogging shoes to commit us to our goal: physical fitness. But many of us have to admit that at some point, our goals shift and we find ourselves spending less and less time in "exercise mode."

With that in mind, we can see why Paul told the Corinthians, "Run in such a way as to get the prize." It's very easy to let our daily Divine Training Program slide a little bit. That's why we must learn to become good soldiers of Jesus Christ, living lives of victory. A hit-or-miss approach to our relationship with God will not yield such a powerful result. Just as with the painful realities of physical training, we have to commit to a goal.

A new program or method may not create that commitment. (Like the new exercise machine, it may lie unused in a corner, too.) So, how can we possibly run, train, exercise ourselves spiritually in such a way as to get the prize? If we so often fail at physical training programs, we know the spirit is willing but the flesh is weak! What can we do? Did God set us up, doomed always to clutch after a life of victory, feeling guilty over our failures or spiritually superior over our successes?

God didn't set us up. It's just that in our decisions to *do something,* we sometimes forget this vital truth: Having begun our lives in Jesus by the power of His Spirit, we must remember that the only way to keep up the pace, to stay in shape, is by that *same* Power! In John 15:5, Jesus told His closest friends, "Without Me, you can do nothing" (*NKJV*). Consistent, powerful time spent with God can *only* come through *His* power . . . not ours! And He is always waiting and able to help us! When we want to stay in bed or skip devotions today, He's waiting. We need to remember to stop and say, "Lord, without You I can't do this. Please make me able to get up, to pray, to spend time with You. I know I am dependent on You, Lord. Please do whatever You need to do in me so I am able!"

Top-notch spiritual condition, ready for whatever God wants us to do, is an attainable goal—if we commit to asking Him to make us able.

In short, [non-discipleship] costs exactly that abundance of life
Jesus said he came to bring.
DALLAS WILLARD

getting your spiritual life in shape

starter

GOALS: Goals are important. If you don't have goals, how will you know if you've accomplished what you want to be and do in life? Check the answer that describes best what your goals in life are.

- ☐ Unclear
- ☐ Seldom obtained
- ☐ A real priority
- ☐ What goals?
- ☐ Clear
- ☐ Achieved regularly

Note: You can download this group study guide in 8¹/₂" x 11¹/₂" format at **www.gospellight.com/uncommon/prayer_and_the_devotional_life.zip.**

Here is an important exercise in goal setting. Write out a short-term (in one year) goal and a long-term (five to seven years) goal for each area of your life listed below.

1. Spiritual Goals

    Short-term (1 year):

    _____

    _____

    _____

    _____

    Long-term (5-7 years):

    _____

    _____

    _____

    _____

2. Relationship Goals (family and friends)

    Short-term (1 year):

    _____

    _____

    _____

    _____

    Long-term (5-7 years):

    _____

    _____

    _____

    _____

3. School or Career Goals

Short-term (1 year):

....

....

....

....

Long-term (5-7 years):

....

....

....

....

message

Once we know where we're headed, we have to figure out what we
need along the way. The apostle Paul gave the church in Ephesus
a list of what they would need in their spiritual journey in Ephesians 6:11-18. As you read this passage, consider the following
questions: (1) Who does Paul state our struggle is against? (2) How
are each of the items in his list like putting on armor? (3) What
does he say about prayer?

*Put on the full armor of God so that you can take your stand
against the devil's schemes. For our struggle is not against flesh and
blood, but against the rulers, against the authorities, against the
powers of this dark world and against the spiritual forces of evil in
the heavenly realms. Therefore put on the full armor of God, so that
when the day of evil comes, you may be able to stand your ground,*

and after you have done everything, to stand. Stand firm then, with the belt of truth buckled around your waist, with the breastplate of righteousness in place, and with your feet fitted with the readiness that comes from the gospel of peace. In addition to all this, take up the shield of faith, with which you can extinguish all the flaming arrows of the evil one. Take the helmet of salvation and the sword of the Spirit, which is the word of God. And pray in the Spirit on all occasions with all kinds of prayers and requests. With this in mind, be alert and always keep on praying for all the saints.

1. Draw the armor of God on the person below.

2. How is each piece of armor used in a spiritual battle?

Belt of truth:

_____

_____

_____

Breastplate of righteousness:

_____

_____

_____

Shoes of the gospel of peace:

_____

_____

_____

Shield of faith:

_____

_____

_____

Helmet of salvation:

_____

_____

_____

Sword of the Spirit:

_____

_____

_____

_____

_____

3. Getting our spiritual life in shape is all about suiting up
    in the armor of God. Each of these areas is a necessary as-
    pect of spiritual fitness. In which area do you feel strong
    and well equipped? What have you been doing to get that
    area into shape?

_____

_____

_____

_____

_____

4. In which area do you feel weaker and ill equipped? What
    have you *not* been doing to allow that area to weaken?

_____

_____

_____

_____

_____

dig

How do we go about arming ourselves in God's armor, and becoming spiritually fit? Paul had some ideas about that, too: "Do

you not know that in a race all the runners run, but only one gets the prize? Run in such a way as to get the prize. Everyone who competes in the games goes into strict training. They do it to get a crown that will not last; but we do it to get a crown that will last forever. Therefore I do not run like a man running aimlessly; I do not fight like a man beating the air. No, I beat my body and make it my slave so that after I have preached to others, I myself will not be disqualified for the prize" (1 Corinthians 9:24-27).

In a way, 1 Corinthians 9:24-27 is Paul's philosophy of life. It could be summed up like this: "There is the easy road to life that gets you nowhere and there is the disciplined road that leads to spiritual victory. Choose the disciplined road."

Many Christians let their spiritual lives get out of shape. They get lazy and don't exercise their spiritual muscles and their relationships with God become shallow. If you desire to get your spiritual life in shape, take a closer look at Paul's philosophy of life.

1. What type of race is Paul describing?

_____

_____

_____

_____

2. What race are you facing?

_____

_____

_____

_____

_____

3. What will it take to win your race?

4. What does discipline have to do with it, according to this passage?

5. In your own words, describe the principle Paul shared with Timothy in 1 Timothy 4:7.

6. How do "myths and old wives' tales" relate to the magical ideas our culture sells about success without hard work?

7. What common elements are there in an athlete's discipline and spiritual discipline?

    ....

    ....

    ....

    ....

    ....

8. What was Paul's goal?

    ....

    ....

    ....

    ....

9. What is your goal?

    ....

    ....

    ....

    ....

    ....

apply

1. Most Christians want to become more spiritually fit, but many don't. What are some things that keep them from developing spiritual discipline?

    ....

    ....

    ....

    ....

2. What does this phrase mean: "He or she who aims at nothing gets there every time"?

3. Who do you know who has his or her spiritual life in shape? What steps did he or she take to get in shape?

4. What characteristics do you see in his or her life that show you his or her spiritual fitness?

5. Consider talking with that person this week about his or her "fitness program." What are three questions you will ask about how he or she stays spiritually fit?

   1.

   2.

3. _____

_____

_____

reflect

1. In Colossians 3:17, Paul writes, "And whatever you do, whether in word or deed, do it all in the name of the Lord Jesus, giving thanks to God the Father through him." According to this verse, how much of your time and attention does God want?

_____

_____

_____

_____

_____

_____

2. How much of your time and attention does God have in each of these areas?

	All of it	Most of it	Some of it	None of it
Prayer	❏	❏	❏	❏
Bible reading	❏	❏	❏	❏
Living like a servant	❏	❏	❏	❏
Giving	❏	❏	❏	❏
Friendships	❏	❏	❏	❏
Sharing Christ with others	❏	❏	❏	❏
Loving your family	❏	❏	❏	❏

3. Make a commitment to do one thing this week to improve each area of your spiritual fitness. Share your commitment with a friend to keep each other accountable.

Prayer:

_____

_____

_____

_____

_____

Bible reading:

_____

_____

_____

_____

_____

Living like a servant:

_____

_____

_____

_____

_____

Giving:

_____

_____

_____

_____

_____

Friendships:

_____

_____

_____

_____

Sharing Christ with others:

_____

_____

_____

_____

Loving your family:

_____

_____

_____

_____

meditation

Do you not know that in a race all the
runners run, but only one gets the prize?
Run in such a way as to get the prize.

1 CORINTHIANS 9:24

HOME **HW** WORI

Get Equipped with HomeWord...

LISTEN
HomeWord Radio
programs reach over 800 communities nationwide with *HomeWord with Jim Burns* – a daily ½ hour interview feature, *HomeWord Snapshots* – a daily 1 minute family drama, and *HomeWord this Week* – a ½ hour weeken edition of the daily program, and our one-hour program.

CLICK
HomeWord.com
provides advice and resources to millions of visitors each year. A truly interactive website, HomeWord.com provides access to parent newsletter, Q&As, online broadcasts, tip sheets, our online store and more.

READ
HomeWord Resources
parent newsletters, equip families and Churches worldwide with practical Q&As, online broadcasts, tip sheets, our online store and more. Many of these resources are also packaged digitally to meet the needs of today's busy parents.

ATTEND
HomeWord Events
Understanding Your Teenager, Building Healthy Morals & Values, Generation 2 Generation and Refreshing Your Marriage are held in over 100 communities nationwide each year. HomeWord events educate and encourage parents while providing answers to life's most pressing parenting and family questions.

A Ministry with *Jim Burns*

In response to the overwhelming needs of parents and families, Jim Burns founded HomeWord in 1985. HomeWord, a Christian organization, equips and encourages parents, families, and churches worldwide.

Small Group Curriculum Kits

Confident Parenting Kit

This is a must-have resource for today's family! Let Jim Burns help you to tackle overcrowded lives, negative family patterns, while creating a grace-filled home and raising kids who love God and themselves.

Kit contains:
- 6 sessions on DVD featuring Dr. Jim Burns
- CD with reproducible small group leader's guide and participant guides
- poster, bulletin insert, and more

Creating an Intimate Marriage Kit

Dr. Jim Burns wants every couple to experience a marriage filled with A.W.E.: affection, warmth, and encouragement. He shows husbands and wives how to make their marriage a priority as they discover ways to repair the past, communicate and resolve conflict, refresh their marriage spiritually, and more!

Kit contains:
- 6 sessions on DVD featuring Dr. Jim Burns
- CD with reproducible small group leader's guide and participant guides
- poster, bulletin insert, and more

Parenting Teenagers for Positive Results

This popular resource is designed for small groups and Sunday schools. The DVD features real family situations played out in numorous family vignettes followed by words of wisdom by youth and family expert, Jim Burns, Ph.D.

Kit contains:
- 6 sessions on DVD featuring Dr. Jim Burns
- CD with reproducible small group leader's guide and participant guides
- poster, bulletin insert, and more

Teaching Your Children Healthy Sexuality Kit

Trusted family authority Dr. Jim Burns outlines a simple and practical guide for parents on how to develop in their children a healthy perspective regarding their bodies and sexuality. Promotes godly values about sex and relationships.

Kit contains:
6 sessions on DVD featuring Dr. Jim Burns
CD with reproducible small group leader's guide and participant guides
poster, bulletin insert, and more

HOME WORD
WHERE PARENTS GET REAL ANSWERS

Parent and Family Resources from HomeWord
for you and your kids...

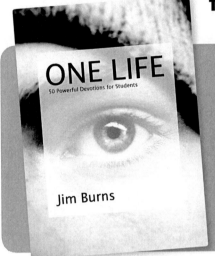

One Life Kit
Your kids only have one life – help them discover the greatest adventure life has to offer! 50 fresh devotional readings that cover many of the major issues of life and faith your kids are wrestling with such as sex, family relationships, trusting God, worry, fatigue and daily surrender. And it's perfect for you and your kids to do together!

Addicted to God Kit
Is your kids' time absorbed by MySpace, text messaging and hanging out at the mall? This devotional will challenge them to adopt thankfulness, make the most of their days and never settle for mediocrity! Fifty days in the Scripture is bound to change your kids' lives forever.

Devotions on the Run Kit
These devotionals are short, simple, and spiritual. They will encourage you to take action in your walk with God. Each study stays in your heart throughout the day, providing direction and clarity when it is most needed.

90 Days Through the New Testament Kit
Downloadable devotional. Author Jim Burns put together a Bible study devotional program for himself to follow, one that would take him through the New Testament in three months. His simple plan was so powerful that he was called to share it with others. A top seller!

Tons of helpful resources for youth workers, parents and youth. Visit our online store at www.HomeWord.com or call us at 800-397-9725

HOME WORI
WHERE PARENTS GET REAL ANSWEI

Small Group Curriculum Kits

Confirming Your Faith Kit

Rite-of-Passage curriculum empowers youth to make wise decisions...to choose Christ. Help them take ownership of their faith! Lead them to do this by experiencing a vital Christian lifestyle.

Kit contains:
- 13 engaging lessons
- Ideas for retreats and special Celebration
- Solid foundational Bible concepts
- 1 leaders guide and 6 student journals (booklets)

0 Building Blocks Kit

earn to live, laugh, love, and play together as a family. 'hen you learn the 10 essential principles for creating happy, close-knit household, you'll discover a family at shines with love for God and one another! Use this irriculum to help equip families in your church.

it contains:
10 sessions on DVD featuring Dr. Jim Burns
CD with reproducible small group leader's guide and participant guides
poster and bulletin insert
10 Building Blocks book

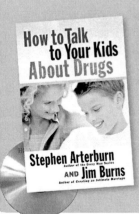

How to Talk to Your Kids About Drugs Kit

Dr. Jim Burns speaks to parents about the important topic of talking to their kids about drugs. You'll find everything you need to help parents learn and implement a plan for drug-proofing their kids.

Kit contains:
- 2 session DVD featuring family expert Dr. Jim Burns
- CD with reproducible small group leader's guide and participant guides
- poster, bulletin insert, and more
- How to Talk to Your Kids About Drugs book

uncommon

high school group studies

the Christian life
ISBN 08307.46447
ISBN 978.08307.46446

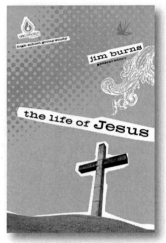

the life of Jesus
ISBN 08307.47265
ISBN 978.08307.47269

resisting temptation
ISBN 08307.47893
ISBN 978.08307.47894

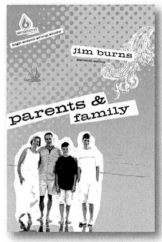

parents & family
ISBN 08307.50975
ISBN 978.08307.50979

uncommon
leaders' resources

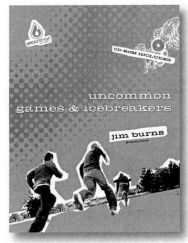

uncommon games & icebreakers

Jim Burns, General Editor
Manual w/ CD-ROM
ISBN 978.08307.46354

uncommon object lessons & discussion starters

Jim Burns, General Editor
Manual w/ CD-ROM
ISBN 978.08307.50986

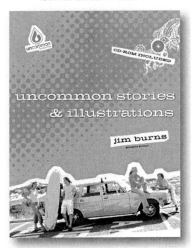

uncommon stories & illustrations

Jim Burns, General Editor
Manual w/ CD-ROM
ISBN 978.08307.47252

uncommon dramas, skits & sketches

Jim Burns, General Editor
Manual w/ CD-ROM
ISBN 978.08307.47917